The Burrell Collection
WESTERN ASIATIC ANTIQUITIES

THE BURRELL COLLECTION

Western Asiatic Antiquities

Edgar Peltenburg

EDINBURGH UNIVERSITY PRESS

for The Burrell Collection · Glasgow Museums

© Edgar Peltenburg, 1991
Edinburgh University Press
22 George Square, Edinburgh

Typeset in Lasercomp Ehrhardt, and
printed in Great Britain by
The Alden Press, Oxford.

British Library Cataloguing-in-Publication Data
Western Asiatic antiquities: The Burrell
Collection.
  I. Peltenburg, Edgar
  933

  ISBN 0-7486-0224-0 (cased)

Contents

Preface

The art of Western Asia, where some of the earliest cultural and artistic activities of the ancient world occurred, is represented in the Burrell Collection by a wide and fairly comprehensive coverage.

The various artefacts provide evidence for craftmanship and in some cases have historical significance. The early periods of Mesopotamian culture are shown by Sumerian statuettes, stone animal vases, stamp seals and amulets. The pieces of relief sculpture which once formed part of a series of wall slabs decorating the palaces of Assyrian kings are a direct link to historical and biblical periods. Contemporary with the Assyrians were the inhabitants of Luristan in Western Iran, famous for the production of a range of bronze work such as horse trappings, standards, implements and vessels which form an important section of the collection. A few items from Cyprus give a hint of the ancient art of this island with its close ties and trade links with the Asiatic mainland.

The catalogue will bring together this part of Sir William Burrell's Collection and present it in a comprehensive form of interest and use to layman and scholars alike. In having Dr. Edgar Peltenburg to write the catalogue, Glasgow Museums and the Burrell Collection in particular have been fortunate in obtaining the service of a scholar of international repute.

Rosemary Watt
Keeper *Burrell Collection.*

INTRODUCTION and
ACKNOWLEDGMENTS

This catalogue presents all the little known objects from early Western Asia in the Burrell Collection. By Western Asia is meant the present Middle Eastern countries of Iran, Iraq, Syria, Turkey, Lebanon, Jordan, Israel and Cyprus. In spite of the absence of great extant monuments, and the corresponding lower profile which this region has in the public consciousness than the neighbouring country Egypt for example, some of man's greatest achievements were wrought here. Modern man is the heir to many of them. In this region the first successful steps were taken from a mobile foraging and hunting existence to a settled agricultural life style and from villages to large centres of population. Eventually, pristine urban societies developed in Mesopotamia (Iraq), with many of the features – specialization, literacy, institutionalized governmental agencies, monumental buildings – that characterize many of our own urbanized circumstances.

It is increasingly clear that secondary states evolved during the Bronze Age in regions bordering the Mediterranean, in part as a result of the desire of elite native groups to emulate and adapt what they had seen or heard about in Mesopotamia and Egypt. This highly selective transmission was coupled with local developments. It led to the formation of distinct polities which nonetheless shared many socioeconomic traditions. They are found in Anatolia, in Biblical lands, in Canaanite kingdoms and in Phoenicia; and they are ultimately recognizable in our own societies.

Insights into many of these processes of human development are preserved in the small works of art that typify Western Asiatic civilisations. The monumental structures of Mesopotamia were largely fashioned of mud brick, unlike the stone monuments of Egypt, and hence they have not survived well. More durable and less spectacular small artefacts, in particular the cuneiform tablets, constitute our primary sources of information. With its minor works of representational art, the Burrell Collection is thus well placed to reflect and inform about critical advances in man's early history.

The Western Asiatic antiquities presented here constitute but a small section of Sir William Burrell's collection, a size that is to be accounted for by his belated interest in this field. Acquisition dates of relevant objects reveal that he only took an active interest in Western Asia from the late 1940s, when he was an octogenarian. Nonetheless this part of his collection is one of the largest and certainly the most representative of its kind in Scotland. It ranks among the major ancient Western Asiatic assemblages in the United Kingdom and it is chiefly notable for its Sumerian votive figurines, Neo-Assyrian relief sculptures and "Luristan" bronzes. Other cultures and areas that figure in it include Babylonia, Urartu in Anatolia, Achaemenid Persia, Cyprus and the Levantine mainland during the Bronze and Iron Ages. Many of the objects are of historical significance and they are not as well known as they deserve to be. This Catalogue therefore is an attempt to bring them to the notice of a wider public, lay and scholarly alike.

When requested by Mr William Wells, the former Keeper of the Burrell Collection, to catalogue these objects, I naturally felt honoured, yet two persistent reservations lingered in my mind: the ethics of apparently supplying a seal of approval to collecting habits which promote the destruction of archaeological evidence, and the ability of one person to deal satisfactorily with so heterogeneous an assemblage.

In answer to the first, I was aware that some pieces suspected of being forgeries were already being published as authentic, so seriously misleading public understanding and scholarly endeavour. One urgent task therefore was to rectify published information and prevent further misuse of these artefacts by rigorous stylistic and scientific analyses. The more general ethical question was confronted by admitting the reality of the case. Many objects existed without contextual information, yet their publication could still contribute to a better understanding of the nature and evolution of some of the earliest known civilisations. To publish is not to condone the unregulated trade in antiquities: indeed, it will be seen in the Catalogue commentaries that a meaningful understanding of many of the objects considered here is frustrated time and again by the lack of full contextual information. This damaging shortfall should be regarded as a clarion call for modern collections to be obtained from scientifically controlled and approved excavations, with full stratigraphic and contextual information attached to each object.

Ideally each group of objects, and in some cases single objects, from the many distinctive cultures represented here should be dealt with by a specialist in the relevant field. To meet the second reservation mentioned above, and to overcome deficiencies in my original ascriptions and commentaries, I requested and was willingly given help and advice by many colleagues. I am grateful to all of these, particularly to P.R.S. Moorey for his comments and for reading a first draft of the Catalogue, and to E. Bleibtreu, A. Caubet, J.C. Courtois, S. Dalley, V. Karageorghis, O. Masson, T.C. Mitchell, C. Phillips, G. Philip, S. Pickles, J. Reade, St. John Simpson, A. Spycket, F. Tallon, V. Tatton-Brown and T. Watkins for varied assistance. Mr. J.K. Thomson, Depute Keeper of The Burrell Collection, unfailingly supplied essential information with efficiency and promptness. Dr B. Bluck and Miss J. Porter identified stones, many of them by X-Ray Diffraction analysis. Dr. P. Wilthew disrupted his schedule in order to examine and report on selected metals at short notice. Mrs. S. Stevenson crafted the line drawings and Mr. J. Stewart the photos. For what remains, I alone am responsible.

Figures 14b and 14c (Musée du Louvre/AO 19807 and 19808) are reproduced with permission of Musée du Louvre. Figure 16 is reproduced with permission of Deutsches Archäologisches Institut Abt. Baghdad.

NOTES TO THE CATALOGUE

In order to present such a diverse collection in an intelligible manner to interested non-specialists, the entries for groups of objects assigned to a particular culture or region are preceded by brief notes on the cultural and historical background to that group. In such cases where there exists an important and coherent sub-group of objects, as in the case of Sumerian worshipper statuettes, additional notes on the role of such objects in society are supplied as introductions. Individual entries comprise Catalogue number, object title, Burrell Collection number, period and/or date, provenance if any, my suggested provenance (here or in the commentaries), measurements, publication reference if any and acquisition source and date. There is little accurate documentation regarding the provenance of objects. Sir William occasionally transferred information from dealers to photos or cards, but as such information is regarded as virtually worthless, the ascription "unprovenanced" is used for those cases. Dr. R.D. Barnett made a preliminary assessment of this part of the collection before it was transferred to its Pollok Country Park premises, and while I am indebted to him for many of his suggestions concerning date and possible source, this information is not used as an indication of provenance. The commentaries that follow Catalogue entries are designed more with the specialist in mind, as are the metal analyses in the two Appendices.

List of References

ADAMS, R
1981   *Heartland of Cities.* London.

AKURGAL, EKREM
1949   *Spaethethitische Bildkunst.* Ankara.

AMANDRY, P
1956   Chaudrons á protomes de taureau en Orient et en Grèce, *in* Saul S Weinberg (ed.), *The Aegean and The Near East*, 239-61. New York.

1959   Toreutique achéménide, *Antike Kunst* 2, 38-56.

AMIET, P
1966   *Elam.* Anvers-sur-Oise.

1972   *Glyptique Susienne (Memoires de la Delégation Archéologique en Iran 43)* Paris.

1986   *L'âge des échanges inter-iraniens 3500-1700 avant J.-C.* Paris.

ANDERSON, W G
1986   *Sarepta I. The Late Bronze and Iron Age Strata of Area II. Y.* Beyrouth.

ANDRAE, W
1922   *Die Archaischen Ischtar-Tempel in Assur (Wissenschaftliche Veröffentlichungen der Deutschen Orient-Gesellschaft 39)* Leipzig.

1935   *Die Jüngeren Ischtar-Tempel in Assur (Wissenschaftliche . . . . . 58)* Leipzig.

ASHMOLEAN
B Buchanan, P R S Moorey (eds), *Catalogue of Ancient Near Eastern Seals in the Ashmolean Museum II The Prehistoric Stamp Seals.* Oxford, 1984.

AZARPAY, G
1968   *Urartian Art and Artifacts. A Chronological Study.* Berkeley.

BADRÉ, L
1980   *Les figurines anthropomorphiques en terre cuite à l'âge du bronze en Syrie.* Paris.

BARNETT, R D
1976   *Sculptures from the North Palace of Ashurbanipal at Nineveh (668-627BC).* London.

BARRELET, MARIE-THÉRÈSE
1968   *Figurines et reliefs en terre cuite de la Mésopotamie antique. I.* Paris.

BASS, G F
1987   Oldest Known Shipwreck Reveals Splendors of the Bronze Age, *National Geographic Magazine* 172, 693-734.

BEHM BLANCKE, M

1979   *Das Tierbild in der Altmesopotamischen Rundplastik (Baghdader For-
schung 1)* Mainz am Rhein.

BEYER, D (ED.)

1982   *Meskéné-Emar. Dix ans de travaux 1972-1982.* Paris.

BOEHMER, R M

1965   Zur Datierung der Nekropole von Tepe Sialk, *Archäologischer
Anzeiger* 802-22.

BOESE, J

1971   *Altmesopotamische Weihplatten: eine sumerische Denkmalsgattung des 3.
Jahrtausends v. Chr.* Berlin.

BÖRKER-KLÄHN, J

1972   Haartrachten, *Reallexikon der Assyriologie* IV, 1-12.

BRAUN-HOLZINGER, E A

1977   *Frühdynastische Beterstatuetten.* Berlin.

1984   *Figurliche Bronzen aus Mesopotamien (Prähistorische Bronzefunde* I. 4)
Munich.

1988   Bronze Objects from Babylonia, *in* Curtis 1988, 119-34.

1989   REC 447-LÁ = Libations becher, *Zeitschrift für Assyriologie* 79, 1-7.

BREASTED, J H

1906   *Ancient Records of Egypt I-V.* Chicago.

BRINKMAN, J A

1976   *Materials and Studies for Kassite History* I. Chicago.

BRUSSELS

De Sumer á Babylone. Brussels, 1983.

BUREN, E D VAN

1931   *Foundation Figurines and Offerings.* Berlin.

1948   Fish-Offerings in Ancient Mesopotamia, *Iraq* 10, 101-22.

CAD

Chicago Assyrian Dictionary. Chicago, 1956-present.

CALMEYER, P

1965   Eine westiranische Bronzewerkstatt . . . , *Berliner Jahrbuch für Vor-
und-Frügeschichte* 5, 1-65.

1969   *Datierbare Bronzen aus Luristan und Kirmanshah.* Berlin.

1970   Federkranze und Musik, in *Actes de la XVIII Recontre Assyriologique
Internationale,* 184-95.

CAMPBELL THOMPSON, R C

1903   *Devils and Evil Spirits of Babylonia* I. London.

1933   The British Museum Excavations at Nineveh, 1931–32, *Liverpool
Annals of Archaeology and Anthropology* 20, 71–186.

CARTER, H & NEWBERRY, P

1904   *The Tomb of Thutmosis IV.* London.

CATLING, H W
    1964   *Cypriot Bronzework in the Mycenaean World*. Oxford.

COCQUERILLAT, D
    1952   Les masses d'armes d'aprés les textes, *Revue d'Assyriologie* 47, 121-36.

COLLEDGE, M A R
    1967   *The Parthians*. London.

CONTENAU, G
    1931   *Manuel d'archéologie orientale* II. Paris.

    1941   Monuments, *Revue d'Assyriologie* 38, 44-56.

    1947   *Manuel d'archéologie orientale* IV. Paris.

COURTOIS, J-C
    1983   La trésor de poids de Kalavassos-Ayios Dhimitrios 1982, *Report of the Department of Antiquities, Cyprus* 117-30.

    1984   *Alasia III. Les objets des niveaux stratifiés d'Enkomi*. Paris.

COWELL, M
    1977   Energy dispersive x-ray fluorescence analyses of ancient gold alloys, *PACT* 1, 76-85.

CRADDOCK, P T
    1978   Europe's earliest brasses, *MASCA Journal*, 1,1.

    1980   The first brass: some early claims reconsidered, *MASCA Journal*, 1, 4.

CRADDOCK, P T & MEEKS, N D
    1987   Iron in ancient copper, *Archaeometry* 29, 2, 187-204.

CULICAN, W
    1961   The First Merchant Venturers, *in* Stuart Piggot (ed.) *The Dawn of Civilization*. London.

    1965   *Medes and Persians*. London.

    1971   Two Syrian Objects from Egypt, *Levant* 3, 86-9.

    1975   Syro-Achaemenian Ampullae, *Iranica Antiqua* 11, 100-112.

CURTIS, J
    1982   *Fifty Years of Mesopotamian Discovery*. London.

    1983   Some Axe-heads from Chagar Bazar and Nimrud *Iraq* 45, 73-81.
(ED.)
    1988   *Bronze-working Centres of Western Asia* c *1000-539 BC*. London.

    1989   *Excavations at Qasrij Cliff and Khirbet Qasrij*. London.

DALLEY, S
    1934   *Mari and Karana*. London.

DAVIES, N DE GARIS
    1922   *The Tomb of Puyemrê at Thebes*. New York.

DESHAYES, J
    1960   *Les Outils de Bronze de l'Indus au Danube*. Paris.

DUNAND, M
    1937   *Fouilles de Byblos I. Atlas*. Paris.

    1950   *Fouilles de Byblos II*. Paris.

ELLIS, R S

    1968   *Foundation Deposits in Ancient Mesopotamia*. London.

Exh. Glasgow

    1949   Exhibit number at McLellan Galleries, Glasgow.

    1951   Exhibit number at Glasgow Museum and Art Gallery, Kelvingrove.

FRANKEL, D

    1983   *Early and Middle Bronze Age material in the Ashmolean Museum, Oxford (Corpus of Cypriote Antiquities 7: Studies in Mediterranean Archaeology 20:7)* Gothenburg.

FRANKFORT, H

    1939a   *Cylinder Seals. A Documentary Essay on the Art and Religion of the Ancient Near East*. London.

    1939b   *Sculpture of the Third Millennium BC from Tell Asmar and Khafajah (Oriental Institute Publications XLIV)* Chicago.

    1970   *The Art and Architecture of the Ancient Orient*. Harmondsworth.

GADD, C J

    1936   *The Stones of Assyria*. London.

    1948   Two Assyrian Observations, *Iraq* 10, 19-25.

GHIRSHMAN, R

    1966   *Tchoga Zanbil* I (*Memoires de la Delegation Archéologique en Iran* 39) Paris.

GIBSON, M

    1975   *Excavations at Nippur, Eleventh Season (Oriental Institute Communications* 22) Chicago.

GJERSTAD, E

    1960   Pottery Types, Cypro-Geometric to Cypro-Classical, *Opuscula Atheniensia* 3, 105-22.

GLYPTIQUE

    Glyptique No. 508-624. Paris-Drouot Montaigne, 1989. Paris.

GODARD, A

    1965   *The Art of Iran*. London.

GOFF, C

    1978   Excavations at Baba Jan: The Pottery and Metal from Levels III and II, *Iran* 16, 29-65.

GORING, E

    1988   *A Mischievous Pastime*. Edinburgh.

GREEN, A

    1985   A Note on the 'Scorpion-Man and Pazuzu', *Iraq* 47, 75-82.

HAERINCK, E

    1988   The Iron Age in Guilan: proposal for a chronology, *in* Curtis 1988, 63-78.

HALL, H R & WOLLEY, C L

    1927   *Ur Excavations I. Al-'Ubaid*. Oxford.

HALL, H R

1928 *Babylonian and Assyrian Sculpture in the British Museum.* London.

HALLER, A

1954 *Die Gräber und Grüft von Assur (Wissenschaftliche Veröffentlichungen der Deutschen Orient-Gesellschaft* 65) Berlin.

HAMILTON, R W

1935 Excavations at Tell Abu Hawām, *Quarterly of the Department of Antiquities of Palestine* 4, 1-69.

1966 A Silver Bowl in the Ashmolean Museum, *Iraq* 28, 1-17.

HANFMANN, G

1956 Four Urartian Bulls' Heads, *Anatolian Studies* 6, 205-13.

HANNAH, A

1953 Glasgow, *in* Wissenschaftliche Berichte, *Archiv für Orientforschung* 16, 112-113, 349-51.

1956 Glasgow, *in* Wissenschaftliche Berichte, *Archiv für Orientforschung* 18, 185-6, 407-9.

HANSEN, D

1970 A Proto-Elamite Silver Figurine in the Metropolitan Museum of Art, *Metropolitan Museum Journal* 3, 5-26.

HAYES, W C

1959 *The Scepter of Egypt* II. Cambridge, Mass.

HAYWARD

Treasures from the Burrell Collection. Hayward Gallery, London 1975.

HIGGINS, R A

1954 *Catalogue of Terracottas in the Department of Greek and Roman Antiquities, British Museum* I. London.

HEINRICH, E

1936 *Kleinfunde aus den Archaischen Tempelschichten in Uruk.* Berlin.

HERRMANN, H-V

1966 *Die Kessel der orientalisierenden Zeit (Olympische Forschungen* 6) Berlin.

HÔTEL DROUOT,

1972 *Bronzes des Steppes et de l'Iran. Collection D. David Weill.* Paris.

1973 *Collection Fr. -J. Bach.* Paris.

HOWARD, M

1955 Technical description of the Ivory Writing-Boards from Nimrud, *Iraq* 17, 17-20.

HROUDA, B

1962 *Tell Halaf IV. Die Kleinfunde aus Historischer Zeit.* Berlin.

1965 *Die Kulturgeschichte des assyrischen Flachbildes.* Bonn.

1977 *Isin-Išān Bahrīyāt* I (*Bayerische Akademie der Wissenschaft Phil - Hist Kl Abh* 79) Munich.

INGEN, W VAN

1939 *Figurines from Seleucia on the Tigris.* Ann Arbor.

ISMAIL, B

1974   Ein Pazuzu-Kopf aus Ninive, *Sumer* 30, 121-8.

JAMES, E O

1965   *From Cave to Cathedral.* London.

JANTZEN, U

1972   *Ägyptische und Orientalische Bronzen aus dem Heraion von Samos (Samos* VIII) Bonn.

KARAGEORGHIS, V

1969   *Salamis in Cyprus.* London.

KING, L P

1912   *Babylonian Boundary - Stones and Memorial-Tablets in the British Museum.* London.

KOLDEWEY, R

1914   *The Excavations at Babylon.* London.

KOZLOFF, A P *et al*

1986   *More animals in ancient art from the Leo Mildenberg Collection.* Mainz am Rhein.

KÜHNE, H

1978   Das Motiv der nährenden Frau oder Göttin in Vorderasien, in S. Şahin (*et al.*, eds.) *Studien zur Religion und Kultur Kleinasiens, Festschrift für Friederich Karl Dörner*, 504–515. Leiden.

LAMBERG-KARLOVSKY, C C

1988   The 'Intercultural Style' Carved Vessels, *Iranica Antiqua* 23, 45-95.

LAYARD, A H

1853   *The Monuments of Nineveh.* London.

LE BRETON, L

1957   The Early Period at Susa, Mesopotamian Relations, *Iraq* 19, 79-127.

LLOYD, S

1984   *The Archaeology of Mesopotamia from the Old Stone Age to the Persian Conquest.* London.

LOULLOUPIS, M

1979   The Position of the Bull in the Prehistoric Religions of Crete and Cyprus, *Acts of the International Archaeological Symposium 'The Relations Between Cyprus and Crete ca 2000-500 BC'* 215-222. Nicosia.

LOMBARD, P

1981   Poignards en bronze de la Peninsule d'Oman au lér millenaire. Un problème d'influences iraniennes de l'Age du Fer, *Iranica Antiqua* 16, 87-93.

LOUD, G, ALTMAN, C B

1938   *Khorsabad* II (*Oriental Institute Publications* XL) Chicago.

MALLOWAN, M E L

1947   Excavations at Brak and Chagar Bazar, *Iraq* 9.

1966   *Nimrud and its Remains.* London.

MARKS, R *et al*

1983   *The Burrell Collection.* Glasgow.

MASSON, O

1961   *Les Inscriptions Chypriotes Syllabiques.* Paris.

MAXWELL-HYSLOP, R

1949   Western Asiatic Shaft-Hole Axes, *Iraq* 11, 90-130.

MCLELLAN GALLERIES

The Burrell Collection - Early Civilisations. Glasgow, n.d.

MEUSZYNSKI, J

1976a   Die Reliefs von Assurnasirapli II, *Archäologischer Anzeiger* 423-80.

1976b   Some Reliefs from the North-West Palace at Kalhu, *Études et travaux* 9, 625.

1981   *Die Rekonstruktion der Reliefdarstellungen und ihrer Anordnung in Nordwestpalast von Kalhu (Nimrud) (Baghdader Forschungen 2)* Mainz am Rhein.

MIROSCHEDJI, P de

1973   Vases et objets en steatite susiens du musée du Louvre, *Delegation Archéologique Français en Iran* 3, 9-80.

MOOREY, P R S

1965   A Bronze "Pazuzu" Statuette from Egypt, *Iraq* 27, 33-41.

1971   *Catalogue of the ancient Persian bronzes in the Ashmolean Museum.* Oxford.

1974   *Ancient Persian Bronzes in the Adam Collection.* London.

1985   *Materials and Manufacture in Ancient Mesopotamia (British Archaeological Reports, International Series 237)* Oxford.

MOOREY, P R S & LAMBERT, W G

1972   An Inscribed Bronze Vessel from Luristan, *Iran* 10, 161-3.

MOOREY, P R S & SCHWEIZER, F

1972   Copper and copper alloys in ancient Iraq, Syria and Palestine: some new analyses, *Archaeometry* 14, 177-98.

MOORTGAT, A

1940   *Vorderasiatische Rollsiegel.* Berlin.

1969   *The Art of Ancient Mesopotamia.* London.

MUSCARELLA, O

1974   The Iron Age at Dinkha Tepe, Iran, *Metropolitan Museum Journal* 9, 35-90.

(ED.)

1981a   *Ladders to Heaven. Art Treasures from Lands of the Bible.* Toronto.

1981b   Surkh Dum at the Metropolitan Museum of Art: A Mini-Report, *Journal of Field Archaeology* 8, 327-59.

1988a   The Background to the Luristan Bronzes, *in* Curtis 1988, 33-44.

1988b   *Bronze and Iron Age Near Eastern Artifacts in the Metropolitan Museum of Art.* New York.

NAGEL, W
    1963   *Altorientalisches Kunsthandwerk*. Berlin.

NEGAHBAN, E O
    1964   *A Preliminary Report on Marlik Excavation, Gohar Rud Expedition*. Teheran.

NEWBERRY, P
    1923   *Beni Hasan* I. London.

ÖZGEN, E & ÖZGEN, I
    1988   *Antalya Museum*. Ankara.

PALEY S
    1976   *King of the World. Ashur-nasir-pal II of Assyria 883-859 B.C.* Brooklyn.

PARROT, A
    1948   *Tello: vingt campagnes de fouilles 1877-1933*. Paris.

    1954a Acquisitions et inédits du musée du Louvre, *Syria* 31, 1-13.

    1954b Les fouilles de Mari, neuvième campagne, *Syria* 31, 151-71.

    1956   *Mission Archéologique de Mari I. Le temple d'Ishtar*. Paris.

    1958   *Mission Archéologique de Mari II. Le Palais: Peintures muralles*. Paris.

    1959   *Mission Archéologique de Mari II: Le Palais: Documents et Monuments*. Paris.

    1967   *Mission Archéologique de Mari III. Les temples de Ishtar et de Ninni-zaza*. Paris.

    1968   *Mission Archéologique de Mari IV. Le 'tresor' d'Ur*. Paris.

PATERSON, A
    1912   *Assyrian Sculptures. Palace of Sinacherib*. Den Haag.

PELTENBURG, E J
    1972   On the Classification of Faience Vases from Late Bronze Age Cyprus, *Acts of the First International Congress of Cypriot Studies* 129-36. Nicosia.

PENDLEBURY, J D S
    1951   *The City of Akhenaten* III. London.

PETERS, J
    1898   *Nippur or Explorations and Adventures on the Euphrates* 2. New York.

PICKLES, S
    1988   *Metallurgical Changes in Late Bronze Age Cyprus (Department of Archaeology, Edinburgh University, Occ. Paper* 17) Edinburgh.

PIOTROVSKY, B B
    1967   *Urartu, the Kingdom of Van and its Art*. London.

PK 14
    W Orthmann (ed.) *Der Alte Orient (Propyläen Kunstgeschichte* 14*)* Berlin, 1975.

PORADA, E
    1965   *Ancient Iran*. London.

    1984   The Cylinder Seal from Tell el Dab'a, *American Journal of Archaeology* 88, 485-8.

POPE, A U

    1938   *A Survey of Persian Art from Prehistoric Times to the Present* I-VI. New York.

PRITCHARD, J B

    1954   *The Ancient Near East in pictures relating to the Old Testament*. Princeton (Second edition, 1969).

PULAK, C

    1988   The Bronze Age Shipwreck at Ulu Burun, Turkey: 1985 Campaign, *American Journal of Archaeology* 92, 1-38.

RASHID, S A

    1971   Grundungsbeigaben, in *Reallexikon der Assyriologie* III. Berlin.

READE, J E

    1965   Twelve Ashurnasirpal Reliefs, *Iraq* 27, 119-34.

    1967   Two Slabs from Sennacherib's Palace, *Iraq* 29, 42-8

    1972   The Neo-Assyrian Court and Army: Evidence from the Sculputres, *Iraq* 34, 87-112.

REUTHER, O

    1926   *Die Innenstadt von Babylon (Merkes) (Wissenschaftliche Veröffentlichungen der Deutschen Orient-Gesellschaft* 47) Leipzig.

SCE I-IV

    E. Gjerstad *et al.*, *The Swedish Cyprus Expedition* I-IV (from 1934). Stockholm & Lund.

SCHEIL, V

    1917   Notules XXIII. La pierre GIŠŠIRGALLUM, *Revue d'Assyriologie* 14, 89-91.

SCHLOSSMAN, B L

    1976   Two Foundation Figurines, *Ancient Mesopotamian Art in the Pierpont Morgan Library*. New York.

SEEDEN, H

    1978   Some Old and New Bronzes: True or False, *Berytus* 26, 5-26.

    1980   *The Standing Armed Figurines in the Levant (Prähistorische Bronzefunde* I. 1) Munich.

SEIDL, U

    1988   Urartu as a Bronzeworking Centre, *in* Curtis 1988, 169-75.

SELZ, G

    1983   *Die Bankettszene*. Wiesbaden.

SMITH, S

    1938   *Assyrian Sculptures in the British Museum from Shalmaneser III to Sennacherib*. London.

SOTHEBY'S

    Sotheby's Sales Catalogue (with date). London.

SPYCKET, A

    1981   *La statuaire du proche-orient ancien*. Leiden.

    1988   Lions en terre cuite de Suse, *Iranica Antiqua* 23, 149-62.

STARR, R F S

    1939   *Nuzi* II. Cambridge, Mass.

STERN, E

1982 *Material Culture of the Land of the Bible in the Persian Period 538-332 B.C.* Warminster.

STROMMENGER, E & HIRMER, M

1964 *The Art of Mesopotamia.* London.

TALLON, F

1987 *Métallurgie susienne: de la fondation de Suse au XVIIIe avant J.-C. (Notes et documents des Musées de France, 15)* Paris.

THUREAU-DANGIN, F

1921 Rituel et Amulettes contre Labartu, *Revue d'Assyriologie* 18, 161-98.

TYLECOTE, R F; GHAZNAVI, H A & BOYDELL, P J

1977 Partitioning of trace elements between the ores, fluxes, slags and metal during the smelting of copper, *Journal of Archaeological Science,* 4, 305-33.

UNGER, E

1918 *Katalog der Babylonischen und Assyrischen Sammlung Kaiserlich Osmanische Museen* III. Constantinople.

VANDEN BERGHE, L

1968 Belgische opgravingen en navorsingen in de Pusht-i Kuh, Luristan, *Phoenix* 14, 109-27.

1969 Belgische opgravingen en navorsingen in de Pusht-i Kuh, Luristan, *Phoenix* 15, 267-84.

1970 Belgische opgravingen en navorsingen in de Pusht-i Kuh, Luristan, *Phoenix* 16, 351-66.

1971 La Nécropole de Bard-i Bal en Luristan, *Archéologia* 43, 14-23.

1972a Belgische opgravingen en navorsingen in de Pusht-i Kuh, Luristan, *Phoenix* 18, 121-36.

1972b Recherches archéologiques dans le Luristan, *Iranica Antiqua* 9, 1-48.

1973 Le Luristan á l'âge du fer. La nécropole de Kutal-i-Gulgul, *Archéologia* 65, 16-29.

1987 Les pratiques funeraires á l'âge du Fer III en Pusht-i Kuh, Luristan; les nécropoles genre "War Kabud", *Iraniça Antiqua* 22, 201-66.

VOGEL, K

1959 *Vorgriechische Mathematik* II. Hannover.

WEIDNER, E

1951 Glasgow, *in* Wissenschaftliche Berichte, *Archiv für Orientforschung* 15, 137-8.

WEISS, H (ED.)

1985 *Ebla to Damascus. Art and Archaeology of Ancient Syria.* Washington.

WELLS, W

1958a Glasgow, *in* Wissenschaftliche Berichte, *Archiv für Orientforschung* 18, 164-5, 438.

1958b Bull's Head from Armenia, *Scottish Art Review* 6, 27-8.

1960 Glasgow *in* Wissenschaftliche Berichte, *Archiv für Orientforschung* 19, 189.

WINTER, I J

1986 The King and the Cup, in M Kelly-Buccellati (ed.), *Insight through Images. Studies in Honour of Edith Porada. Bibliotheca Mesopotamica* 21, 253-68. Malibu.

WISEMAN, D J

1955 Assyrian Writing Boards, *Iraq* 17, 3-13.

WOOLLEY, C L

1925 The excavations at Ur, 1923–1924, *Antiquaries Journal* 5, 1–120.

1934 *Ur Excavations II. The Royal Cemetery*. London.

1935 *The Development of Sumerian Art*. London.

1939 *Ur Excavations V. The Ziggurat and its Surroundings*. London.

1956 *Ur Excavations IV: The Early Periods*. London.

1974 *Ur Excavations VI. The Buildings of the Third Dynasty*. London.

1976 *Ur Excavations VII. The Old Babylonian Period*. London.

XANTHOUDIDES, S

1924 *The Vaulted Tombs of the Mesara*. Manchester.

YON, M (ED.)

1987 *Ras Shamra-Ougarit III - La centre de la ville*. Paris.

ZETTLER, R

1987 Sealings as artifacts of institutional administration in Ancient Mesopotamia, *Journal of Cuneiform Studies* 39, 197-240.

Table 1. Chronological Periods of Ancient Western Asia

	SOUTH MESOPOTAMIA	NORTH MESOPOTAMIA	IRAN	LEVANT	ANATOLIA
4000 BC	UBAID				
			SUSA B	CHALCOLITHIC	
	PROTOLITERATE a–b	NORTHERN		SUMERIAN	EARLY
3500 BC	(URUK IV)		C	COLONIES	
	PROTOLITERATE c–d (JEMDAT NASR)	URUK			
3000 BC	EARLY DYNASTIC I			EARLY	BRONZE
	EARLY DYNASTIC II		D		
				BRONZE	
2500 BC	EARLY DYNASTIC III				AGE
	AKKADIAN EMPIRE		SIMASH DYNASTY	AGE	
	THIRD DYNASTY OF UR				
2000 BC	ISIN-LARSA/ OLD BABYLONIAN	OLD ASSYRIAN			ASSYRIAN COLONIES
			SUKKALMAHHU	MIDDLE BRONZE AGE	OLD HITTITE
1500 BC	KASSITE	MITANNIAN EMPIRE			HITTITE EMPIRE
			IRON I MIDDLE ELAMITE	LATE AMARNA BRONZE	
		MIDDLE ASSYRIAN		AGE	
1000 BC			IRON II		NEO-HITTITE STATES
		NEO-ASSYRIAN EMPIRE	NEO-ELAMITE IRON III	PHOENICIAN EXPANSION	URARTU
	NEO-BABYLONIAN EMPIRE			ASSYRIAN	
500 BC				BABYLONIAN	PHRYGIA
	ACHAEMENID PERSIAN	ACHAEMENID PERSIAN	ACHAEMENID PERSIAN	ACHAEMENID PERSIAN	
BC / AD	SELEUCID	SELEUCID	SELEUCID	ANTIGONID SELEUCID	
	PARTHIAN	PARTHIAN	PARTHIAN	ROMAN	ROMAN
	SASSANIAN	SASSANIAN	SASSANIAN	BYZANTINE	BYZANTINE
500 AD					

1 Ancient Near East showing location of sites and areas mentioned in the text.

Black Sea

Caspian Sea

URARTU

• Marlik

• Tepe Sialk

• Persepolis

Persian Gulf

PERSIA

• Hamadan

• Tepe Giyan
• Piravend
Kermanshah •
• Shurabah
Tuttulban • • War Kabud • Baba Jan
Kaleh Nisar • • Tell Agrab • Surkh-i Dum
• Bard-i Bal
• Khafaje Kutal-i Gulgul
Tell Asmar • • Tell Harmal Karkhai
• Selecia • Susa
Jemdat Nasr • • Choga Zanbil
Babylon • Kish ELAM
Nippur • SUMER &
• Bismaya BABYLON
Tello/Girsu • • Lagash
Uruk •
Ubaid • • Ur

DIYALA R.

Toprak Kale •

Hasanlu •

Khorsabad •
Nimrud •
Nineveh •
• Nuzi

ASSYRIA

Tell Brak •
Assur •

• Usiyeh

TIGRIS R.

Tell Chuera •

Harran •
Meskene–Emar •
Mari •

EUPHRATES R.

Çayönü •

Altin Tepe •

Black Sea

Kultepe •

Gordion •

ANATOLIA

Marash •
Sam'al •
Deve Huyuk •
Judeidah •
Iamhad •
Ebla •
Hama •
Massyaf •

Ugarit •
Lapithos •
Salamis •
Arsos • Enkomi
Kalavasos •

CYPRUS

RHODES

SAMOS

Ulu Burun +

MEDITERRANEAN SEA

Byblos •
Akko •
Tell Abu Hawam •
Beth Shan •

JORDAN R.

DEAD SEA

LEVANT

• Teima

Tell Dab'a •
Bubastis •

• Amarna

EGYPT

Red Sea

N

0   200   400   600
KM

I MESOPOTAMIA

Early Mesopotamian Civilisations

The fertile part of modern southern Iraq which lies between Baghdad and the Persian Gulf and is bounded by the Tigris and Euphrates Rivers, a flat alluvial plain of some 10,000 square miles, was once the home of remarkably inventive civilisations (Fig 1).

The Sumerians or 'black-headed people', although long suggested by the Biblical 'land of Shinar', only emerged as a distinct entity in Western consciousness as recently as the late 19th century through the work of philologists and archaeologists. Properly considered, the word Sumerian refers solely to a non-Semitic language, but it has been extended to refer to that mixture of peoples, Semites and aboriginals included, who were responsible for this literate, urbanized and hierarchically organised civilisation which flourished for some one thousand five hundred years, from c 3500 to 2000 BC.

Primarily recorded through curious Greek and usually hostile Biblical accounts, their successors, the Babylonians are slowly being re-established by scientific methods. These started in the late 18th-19th centuries with the explorations of Beauchamp and Rich, for example, and the decipherments of Hincks, Rawlinson and Oppert. Faithful heirs of the Sumerians, the Babylonians were essentially West Semitic nomadic Amorites from the desert fringes who founded a dynasty c 1894 BC in the city of Bab-ilim (See Fig. 1 for location of this and other cities) or the 'gate of the gods' situated in Akkad, to the north of Sumer. Their military power saw but short-lived successes beyond southern Iraq: their civilisation and cultural influence however persisted at least until that very city feebly capitulated to Cyrus the Great of Persia in 539 BC.

The landscape in which these civilisations flourished was demanding. Largely composed of alluvial silt, tracts of water and reed-lined marsh, it is a flat terrain subject to the extremes of desert encroachments caused, for example, by shifting rivers and disastrous floods during harvests. Although its environment was ideal for manageable wildlife such as fish and fowl, it lacks readily definable and defensible borders as well as raw materials like timber and minerals. On a longer time scale, agriculture was beset by salts caused by flood waters and intensive irrigation. Clearly, the key to the successful development of large populations here was a highly organised society in which water management and concentrated agriculture played a critical role. In return for this, the land yielded bountiful crops, especially barley and dates, and it sustained large herds of sheep, goats and cattle. Prosperity fostered the import of required raw materials and rare commodities from India, Afghanistan and the highlands of Iran and Turkey to the gates and quaysides of its cities. Thus it may be seen how the southern Mesopotamian environment was a critical factor in the growth of urban, outward-looking complex societies. To the east of the Tigris River, in the modern Iranian province of Khuzistan, lies an extension of this riverine lowland zone in which the Elamite civilisation developed over an even longer period from c 3500 BC, succumbing finally to the onslaughts of Assyria in the 7th century BC. It shared many cultural characteristics with Sumer and Babylon, often becoming a provincial offshoot of the metropolitan region to its west. This close relationship means that objects in the collection which are attributed in general to the headwaters region of the Persian Gulf could have come from either South Iraq or South West Iran. The unique stone axe, 37, and the suppliant figure of copper, 43, for example, may well have originated in Elam.

The chronology of Babylonian civilisation vies in accuracy with that of the Egyptians and is derived from Greek sources (especially Ptolemy) and cross checks between Mesopotamian king lists, astronomical observations, year names and dated administration texts. The absolute length of years varied, but so exact was the conformity to the annual cycle of rituals that time units were intercalated, thus rendering years approximately equivalent to ours. Until the mid-second millennium BC a year was named after an outstanding event of the preceding year, as in the 19th year of King Shulgi 'Year (in which) the citizens of Ur were organized as spearmen', thereafter by the regnal year of the king, a system which was also adopted by the Persian conquerors: '36th year of Darius, King of Babylon'.

While there are problems of detail in the chronology extending back to the middle of the Kassite Dynasty c 1400 BC there is an outstanding major difficulty regarding the pivotal date of Hammurabi whose Law Code provides such a wealth of social information. This is due to a gap in records between observations of Venus during his Dynasty and the later Kassite documents, thus allowing for a number of alternative proposals for the absolute date of the observation and hence, for Hammurabi himself. His first year is generally placed between 1878 and 1728 and historical chronologies for 500 years before that are shifted accordingly. Earlier still, chronologies are much more inexact and they depend largely on the archaeological principles of stratification, cross-dating and on Carbon-14 determinations. The Middle Chronology, in which Hammurabi's dates are c 1792–1750 BC, is used here.

The Sumerians

Clay tablets with administrative notations in pictographic form first occur c 3500 BC at Uruk, Tell Brak and other sites (Fig 1) and although a thousand years were to elapse before the development of decipherable literature the occurrence of Sumerian words like Enlil (the god of the city Nippur) confirms the presence of this language at such an early date. Pictograms for chariots and boats indicate transport at that time for, amongst other things, wood and copper which were perhaps derived through large-scale Sumerian merchant colonies in North Syria and Anatolia. The earliest writing therefore discloses the existence of a vigorous, sophisticated social infrastructure. Its invention may well have come about because of the increasing complexities of scale caused for example by the need to control the distribution of local agricultural surpluses and foreign commodities. Temple personnel are probably to be included amongst these urbanized elites. Two hallmarks of Early Sumerian civilisation, administrative skills and the central role of temples, are exemplified in this collection by a change from stamp to cylinder seals (1–9), and by elaborate equipment for sacred rituals (15–18). Many objects like these have been found at the city of Uruk which was dominated by monumental halls and temples. It may well be regarded as the hub of the earliest, pristine state. Although it is probable from non-Sumerian words for some indigenous geographical features and crafts that the Sumerians were not natives, or at least not exclusively so, they do seem well established by this time.

In the ensuing centuries administrative buildings and palaces emerge beside the older temples and these are accompanied by the growth of walled cities or 'cult-centres' as they were called. Perhaps as a result of competition for land to feed increased populations, perhaps because of disputes over irrigation rights or for other reasons, conflicts between separatist city-states were endemic by *c* 2500 BC. Warfare with chariots and infantry gave rise to heroic military leaders, or priest-kings referred to as *ens*. The *Sumerian King List*, composed much later from original sources and further copies, is an idealized historical document which deals with this remote period. It is divided into two sections by a 'Flood which swept over (the earth)', a reference no doubt to a period in the earlier part of the 3rd millennium BC when a series of inundations wreaked havoc in southern Iraq. Amongst the *ens* mentioned in the section immediately after the Flood are figures such as Gilgamesh, a 'king' or 'great man' of Uruk, who may have been an historical person of this heroic period of Sumerian civilisation. A somewhat later renowned epic devoted to his quest for everlasting life, a search perhaps reflected in the burial of hosts of servants with their leaders in the contemporary 'Royal' Cemetery at Ur, includes a description of the Flood which is a graphic and detailed model for the Biblical account.

To this Heroic Age may be attributed a series of worshipper figures (22–28), many of them bureaucrats whose very existence affirms the complexities of this earliest literate civilisation. The quality and individuality of male worshipper **25** is such that sculptors must have started to foresake previous anonymity and attempt portraiture, a rare departure in ancient Near Eastern art. Far from a static entity therefore, Sumer comprised several highly competitive city-states that during the Early Dynastic III period (*c* 2600–2350 BC) experienced dynamic change. This led to the formation of one of the most precocious states in antiquity.

About 2350 BC a political and cultural revolution took place under the leadership of the Cup-Bearer of the King of Kish, Sargon, which was his later throne name and simply means 'true king'. The flourishing period (*c* 2350–2150 BC) which this impressive ruler inaugurated is known as the Akkadian Period after his unlocated capital, Agade; the term is also used for the writing of a Semitic dialect, as well as later ones, which now supplanted Sumerian. The focus of power shifted north and Sumer became just one part of a new concept, the Empire. This took Akkadian armies to Syria and Turkey, *ens* were replaced by governors (*ensis*) and independence was replaced by a form of personal centralized bureaucracy which was to stamp its mark deeply on all the following governmental institutions of southern Iraq. Highly personalized leadership of this type is akin to rulership exercised by later, historically attested, tribal sheikhs and its emergence now confirms the heterogeneous character of what we call the Sumerian civilisation. It also accounts for the relative brevity of pre-eminent states subsequently, since power was vested almost exclusively in charismatic leaders.

The end of Sargon's Dynasty was marked by political weakness and the incursion of barbarous Guti and others, who, according to slightly later explanations, came because the Akkadians 'dared assault the Ekur . . . defiled Enlil' by ravaging that god's holy places in Nippur. Some cult-centres however survived intact and one of the most southerly, and hence largely Sumerian, became the capital of an Empire which blended Akkadian ideas of rule with Sumerian piety. This 3rd Dynasty of Ur (2113–2006 BC), shaped by its dynamic founder, Ur-Nammu, is chiefly noted for an early law code, a wealth of administrative texts and monumental building projects which includes a classic ziggurat or temple tower. A foundation figurine, **40**, comes from such a project, probably initiated by one of Ur-Nammu's successors. But this Empire was short-lived, its fabric undermined by the collapse of central authority in the face of growing independence movements of such cities as Isin and attacks by Elamites from the east, Amorites from the west, the latter even necessitating the construction of a protective Long Wall. It was the last, distinctively Sumerian period: thereafter, the language was preserved by scribes, the civilisation's innovations built on and reinterpreted.

Although based on agriculture, Sumerian economy was controlled by city-dwellers. Much of the land was owned by temples, but private property also existed. Large numbers were also employed in textile works which required long term and detailed integration of rural and urban populations. This system was organised in the fortified cities where political power ineluctably moved from an assembly of nobles to individuals, each referred to as a *lugal* or 'big man'. The *lugal* gradually replaced the *en* as the most powerful institution in the Sumerian city-states, and with the introduction of hereditary rule came the formation of kingly dynasties. The rest of secular society consisted of commoners, clients, who were chiefly dependents of temples, nobles and slaves. People were protected from the excesses of bureaucrats and abuses of those in power, such as "the man in charge of fisheries" who seized the fisheries, by reforms and later, law codes promulgated by kings. These were written by scribes who were trained in schools called *edubbas*. They played a unique role in recording court decisions, business transactions, astronomical, mathematical and medicinal texts, poetry and hymns, to name but few. They were needed in international trade, usually carried out in the *kāru* or harbour of these riverine cities where there may have been resident foreign populations.

Just as the towering buildings of monopolistic temple organisations, including the ziggurats set inside their grandiose precincts, overshadowed the physical appearance of Sumerian cities so too did religion most profoundly affect the psychology and daily activities of all individuals. So deeply rooted are religious concepts in Sumerian thought that a detailed, wide ranging religious vocabulary exists which can scarce be understood by Western minds. "Man" so the Babylonian *Epic of Creation* which reflects Sumerian thinking tells us, "shall be charged with the service of the gods". The frequency of mythical subjects, amulets and the like in the Sumerian part of the collection is an apposite expression of how pervasive was the influence of the supernatural in society.

Several objects attributed to ancient Sumer attest to the technical skills of its craftsmen. Metals and hard stones had to be imported, but in spite or perhaps because of this, specialists produced some of the most outstanding works of antiquity in these exotic materials and many inventions may confidently be assigned to ancient Sumer. Metalsmiths were experienced in alloying coppers to produce arsenical and tin-bronzes. The foundation figures **30** and **40**, are probably cast by the lost wax method in which a model of the desired object was first fashioned in wax or other volatile material, enveloped in a clay mould which was heated to melt the model and subsequently filled with molten metal. Upon cooling, the expendable mould was broken to reveal the finished product, free from seams and other blemishes inherent in simpler casting methods. The discovery of the lost wax method of casting bronze took place at least by the Uruk IV period in early Sumer. Moulds were also used to mass produce figurines of pure clay or terracotta. Prior to the late 3rd millennium BC they were hand-made, but with the growth of the demand for such figures (see **41**) moulds were used. Like so many Mesopotamian innovations it was a technique eventually transmitted to Europe. The sophistication of sculptors working in stones which were rare in south Mesopotamia is also evident from many pieces in the collection. This mastery was later recognised in requests from Hittite kings for Babylonian sculptors.

In addition to its chief deity, each city had a plethora of lesser deities and personal names often included the name of a god as one component. An was the heaven god, an old figure whose seat of worship was in Uruk; Enlil, an air god, a most powerful deity who legitimized kings had his temple in Nippur which may account for that city's idiosyncratic history; and Enki the wise god with centres at Uruk and Eridu form the main group of gods. Together with Nin-hursaq, a mother-goddess, Nanna, a moon god, Utu the sun god and Innanna, later Ishtar and Astartu, they are the chief deities of the Sumerian pantheon. Their anthropomorphic statues were fed, bathed and walked in temples. They were perpetually adored by their seemingly insecure servants in the form of statues (22–28), usually of poor quality but richly painted and inlaid.

The Babylonians

After the demise of Sumer, southern Iraq continued as a repository of learning and tradition that persisted to influence the Near East for many centuries. The major internal changes include a concentration of the rule of the 'four quarters of the world' at Babylon, the relegation of the Sumerian language to esoteric works, the widening of political horizons and kingly power, the increasing remoteness of major deities and concomitant proliferation of their symbols, minor deities and demons and the inception, perhaps for political motives, of a national god, Marduk. When Hammurabi, the sixth king of the First Dynasty of Babylon, acceded to the throne c 1792 BC, his was but one of a clutch of vying petty kingdoms. To expand political control, each king needed astute military and diplomatic skills. As one contemporary letter puts it:

'There is no king who by himself is strongest. Ten or fifteen kings follow Hammurabi of Babylon, as many follow Rim-Sin of Larsa, Ibal-pi-el of Eshnunna, and Amut-pi-el of Qatna, while twenty kings follow Yarim-Lim of Iamhad.'

Qatna and Iamhad (modern Aleppo) lay beyond Mesopotamia, in N. Syria. By the end of his reign Hammurabi had united south Mesopotamia and established Babylon as the enduring seat of government.

Political pre-eminence however was ephemeral. The daring and famous raid of the Hittite king Mursilis I (c 1595 BC) destroyed the Old Babylonian empire and ushered in the long rule of the Kassites (c 1500–1157 BC). Their origins are debated but ultimately they effected ultraconservative policies, rebuilding and carrying out traditional duties in the temples. During a period known as the Amarna Age, after the discovery of an Akkadian archive of international correspondence in the Egyptian capital at Amarna, the Kassite Babylonian rulers were included in an exclusive club of Great Kings who addressed each other as 'brothers'. Aside from the Babylonians and Egyptians, these world powers included the Assyrians, Mitanni, Hittites and Alashians (Cypriots). Apart from certain types of seals, glass and terracottas, few notable pieces of Kassite artwork are known and there are none in this collection.

Thereafter, Babylonia was enfeebled by incursions of Aramaeans and the growing militarism of Assyria, intermittent at first, but culminating in the reluctant incorporation of Babylonia into the Assyrian Empire and the ravaging of Babylon itself by Sennacherib in 689 BC. Grasping the opportunity of an exhausted and over-extended Assyria some 60 years later, King Nabopolassar (625–605 BC) succeeded in ejecting Assyria and by allying himself with the Medes took possession of the lowland territories of Assyria. He was a Chaldaean, a tribal group who inhabited the marshes far to the south of Babylon. They kept such accurate records that in Hellenistic times 'Chaldaean' became synonymous with 'astronomer'.

Nabopolassar thus founded the Neo-Babylonian Empire c 625–539 BC which, through Greek and Biblical eyes, presented a fascinating world of Hanging Gardens and Jewish exile after Nebuchadnezzar's capture of Jerusalem in 587 BC. Primary sources of information however are quite inadequate and they deal chiefly with stereotyped building formulae, administrative routines which, nevertheless, do include ration lists for the exiled king Jehoiachin of Judah, astronomical and medical texts and the concise but all too brief historical record, the 'Babylonian Chronicle'. Nebuchadnezzar II (607–562 BC) emerges as an astute exponent of statecraft, an antiquarian and a prolific builder, in part responsible for the immense shimmering Gate of Ishtar, the extensive glazed bricks of which presage their use in later Islamic times. The other principal figure of the period was the much more complex Nabonidus (555–539 BC), the last king of an independent Babylon who candidly said of himself 'I am Nabonidus who has not the honour of being a somebody – kingship is not within me'. His mother was associated with Harran, the major centre for worship of the moon god Sin whose cult he attempted to make paramount in Babylon. About ten years of his reign were spent in remote Teima in Arabia, possibly for reasons of health. Religious fanatic or innovator, neglector of Babylon or putative constructor of a New Babylon at Teima in the safer west on Arabian trade routes, whatever the truth, he was too late to save himself and his regent, the crown prince Belshazzar, and Babylon itself, from an ignominious end. The Persian king, Cyrus, was able to take the city with the statue of its god Marduk marching by his side. With the appointment of a Persian governor, Babylonia became a province in the widened horizons of the new Achaemenid and subsequently the Macedonian Empires.

The Assyrians

Situated in the open rolling countryside of northern Iraq and watered by the Tigris River, its tributaries from the mountains of Kurdistan to the east and sufficient rainfall, Assyria was free from those severely challenging environmental factors which so profoundly affected its southern neighbour, Babylonia. Dry farming, for example, meant that communities were not obliged to undertake the large-scale irrigation works that characterise the south. Possessing a much shorter history which was traced back to tent-dwelling kings in the late 3rd millennium BC, Assyria often looked to Babylonia for cultural, if not political, inspiration. It lacked topographically recognisable borders and so was susceptible to migrating peoples, especially the Hurrians and Aramaeans who threatened Assyria's very existence. The outstanding achievement of the Assyrians however is not that they prevailed as a distinct civilisation in such a perilous situation, but that from a small, often beleaguered homeland they went on to form the world's first enduring and supra-national Empire.

Their history is conventionally divided into Old (c 2000–1742), Middle (c 1385–1045) and Neo-Assyrian (c 900–610 BC) periods, each equating in part with a stage of successful, expansionist policies. The first two were of transient political significance and have left us little monumental art. The Old Assyrian period is chiefly notable because of tablets from Anatolia which disclose that the city of Ashur lay at the hub of an international network of commercial trade in metals, textiles and other commodities. The Assyrian *tamkāru*, or banker, funded merchants' donkey caravans and, by acting as entrepreneurial middleman, reaped enormous profits. With Ashurnasirpal II (883–859 BC) however the foundations of a lasting Empire were laid together with a new artistic expression which first astonished modern Western perceptions in the 1840s upon Botta's and Layard's discoveries of palatial mural reliefs.

With varying fortunes in subsequent reigns, Assyria expanded to conquer Urartu

(714 BC, temporarily), Babylonia (729 BC), Syria (c 731 BC), Israel (721 BC), Judah (701 BC), and for a short time, Egypt (671 BC) and Elam (c 639 BC) in western Iran. Our sources for these events are largely accurate and highly colourful annalistic accounts of the Assyrian kings, historical records replete with minutiae which provide valuable insights into other civilisations. Biblical narratives and Greek and Babylonian sources also refer to the Assyrians sometimes corroborating at other times contradicting the evidence of the Assyrian documents.

As in the cases of the collapse of the earlier Mesopotamian empires of Akkad and the Third Dynasty of Ur, the end of Assyria was marked by invasions from the east, in this case by the Medes. The greatest city of the Ancient Near East, Nineveh, fell in 612 BC. And yet the Medes were more a fatal symptom than the cause of this disaster. Internal crises are already evident in the brevity of the reigns of Ashurbanipal's successors and in the scarcity of monumental buildings and annals after c 627 BC. Assyria, exhausted by fratricidal warfare in Babylonia and its destruction of Elam, over-extended by its Egyptian adventure, stretched by ever decreasing returns from subject territories and expanded bureaucracies and dependant upon foreign mercenaries, was a fragile super power well before 612 BC. What happened to the enormous concentration of population in the Assyrian metropolitan homeland during the ensuing Dark Age is a problem that archaeologists have yet to solve.

The reliefs in the collection come from royal palaces at Nimrud and Nineveh. Although extracted from larger compositions they chronicle some of the major developments of the world's strongest state from the 9th to 6th centuries BC. The emphasis on the supernatural basis of Assyrian kingship and on the incorporation of epic-like annals on the earliest reliefs (45–6) gave way to more numerous depictions of battle scenes (52). As the Empire expanded so too did the various administrative arms of government, epitomized here in the mural with two scribes (47).

Clay and stone stamping devices first appear in early agricultural communities, perhaps in response to the need to mark surplus quantities of stored comestibles. Presumably these were kept and sealed with mud that received the stamp impression. Since the clay or mud was not baked, impressions have not survived. Alternate theories for the development of the seal include simply a decorative use, but it is clear that they were soon employed as administrative tools or to symbolize the ownership of property.

During the 4th millennium BC conical and animal-shaped stamps, perhaps derived from pendants, became widespread in Western Asia. The increasing standardization of seal shapes and drilled designs intimate that they were no longer of purely local significance. Long distance trade was a growing feature of the Near East and its organisation fostered the dissemination of easily recognized types of seals. While they may also have served other or dual roles such as seal and amulet, this dissemination is best explained as a result of evolving trade systems. It is still far from clear how such systems were administered, but when large merchant colonies are first attested, the merchants apply a novel type of seal, the cylinder.

This new device was developed, together with many other innovations, in South Mesopotamia during the fourth millennium BC. When the cylinder was rolled over the soft clay, it imparted its incised design which could now be extended in a continuous frieze. Whether this was considered more practical in order to cover larger areas or whether the dictates of current fashion which so espoused the endless repetition of stock motifs was responsible for the change is unknown. In most areas the cylinder superceded the stamp and it was to become the prevalent type in the Near East for much of antiquity. Many of the earliest cylinders have been found in temples, a sign perhaps of the important commercial role of those great institutions. Early cylinder impressions are found on vessel sealings and bullae, or hollow clay balls containing counters; later they were used extensively to seal important tablets.

Sealstones constitute one of the most uninterrupted sequences of artefact types from the Ancient Near East and, because of their subject matter, precious indicators of religious beliefs, myths and cultural influences. The small collection here belongs to that epochal transition when stamps were gradually replaced by cylinders. The former nonetheless continued to be made as votives or amulets for some time, particularly in provincial centres. They re-appear as conventional stamping devices in the Hittite Empire and during the Iron Age in the Levant. They eventually displaced the traditional cylinder in Mesopotamia itself during the later Neo-Assyrian and Neo-Babylonian periods.

1 Zoomorphic Stamp Seal 28.18

Protoliterate period c 3800–3000 BC. Unprovenanced.

Large flat conoid carved with head of lion in such a way so as to benefit from the yellow veining in the milky white travertine *calcite* which was taken from a stalagmite or stalactite. Pierced longitudinally from both ends; single eye inlaid with polished red stone. Chipped at edges. Short lines consisting of three deep drillings are arranged at random (?) on flat surface.

Height 0.015 m   Length 0.051 m
Max. diameter of bore-holes at surface 0.005 m
Unpublished. Exh. Glasgow 1949, No 144.
Acquired John Hunt, 1948.

2 Zoomorphic Stamp Seal 28.58

Protoliterate period c 3800–3000 BC. Unprovenanced.

Recumbent lioness-shaped body, only the head articulated by modelling and incision; deep eye socket for (lost?) inlay. Plain cream coloured *calcite*. Pierced transversely from both sides. Flat base deeply incised with single animal design (?). Complete.

Height 0.006 m   Length 0.028 m
Max. diameter of bore-holes at surface 0.003–0.005 m
Hannah 1953, 350.17.
Acquired G.F. Williams, 1952.

These zoomorphic stamp seals, robustly and confidently modelled yet cursorily drilled for the stamp, are typical of Susa C where the lion is one of the most popular of the depicted animals (Amiet 1972, Pl 59.434–8). Drilled designs in the Susa repertory include random dots or dots arranged in animal patterns. Virtually identical seals are also common in South Mesopotamia (e.g. Woolley 1955, Pl 38. U.17835A,B) and they reached such sites as Tell Brak in Syria, a major centre that maintained significant contacts with the south (Mallowan 1947, Pl XV). The type therefore is widespread in the later 4th – early 3rd millennia BC and these examples could come from one or more sites in the area stretching from western Iran to Syria.

3 Zoomorphic Stamp Seal 28.57

Protoliterate period c 3800–3000 BC. Unprovenanced.

Body shaped as *couchant* ox-like creature, *regardant*. Cream coloured *calcite and dolomite* with yellow discolouration and small dark flecks. Perforated transversely from both sides. Complete except for chips on base. Flat base has two deeply drilled scorpions (?) and two drillings.

Height 0.016 m   Lenth 0.036 m
Max. diameter of bore-holes at surface 0.004 m
Unpublished.
Acquired G.F. Williams, 1952.

4 Zoomorphic Stamp Seal 28.60

Protoliterate period c 3800–3000 BC. Unprovenanced.

Body shaped as recumbent ox-like creature *regardant*. Deep eye sockets for (lost) inlays. Legs cursorily indicated with unnatural incision at rear. Perforated transversely from both sides. Hard, buff-grey *calcite* complete. Flat base decorated with three groups of central large drillings and tangential lines comprised of smaller drillings, perhaps scorpions or crabs.

Height 0.01 m   Length 0.022 m
Max. diameter of bore-holes at surface 0.002 m
Unpublished.
Acquired G.F. Williams, 1952.

Centres of production for these popular stamp seals modelled in the form of recumbent bovids probably existed in many cities, especially in South Mesopotamia and Elam. Such a southerly, and perhaps more accurately, Sumerian origin for 3 is suggested by the deliberate choice of a speckled stone. In the Uruk 'Sammelfund', which consists of a large number of objects from the temple of the Eanna complex, some animal sculptures were inlaid with floral and other lapis lazuli elements (Heinrich 1936, Pl 13). The seal therefore seems to conform to a peculiar Early Sumerian tradition which eschewed organic unity in preference for a fragmented appearance. That is not to state that the seal was necessarily found in Sumer. The type was also popular in Susa (Amiet 1972, Pl 58.418) and it reached such distant locations as Tell Brak in Syria (*Ashmolean*, No 165). For another with scorpions in

1

2

3

4

5

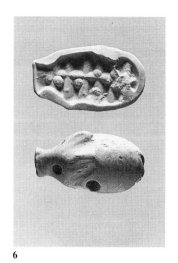

6

7

8

the field see *ibid* No 216. Like **1** and **2** therefore, these seals are likely to have come from one or more sites in the area of western Iran, Iraq or Syria.

5   Zoomorphic Stamp Seal   28.59

Protoliterate period *c* 3800–3000 B C. Unprovenanced.

Body of seal roughly shaped like a recumbent caprid (?). Cursorily executed with a long tail swung over back and anal bore hole; ridge below neck of animal. Cream coloured *marble*; some red veining. Perforated transversely through animal from both sides. Ten drillings on flat base, conceivable in diagonal rows of two, four, three and one. Complete.

Height 0.021 m   Length 0.034 m

Max. diameter of bore-holes at surface 0.006 and 0.004 m

Unpublished.

Acquired G.F. Williams, 1952.

This belongs to a well-known seal type that schematically depicts caprids. Like **1–4**, it mainly occurs in stone such as this and most examples have been found in South Mesopotamian and Elamite contexts of *c* 3000 (*cf* Amiet 1972, Pl 58.418–423). Also, for North Mesopotamia see Mallowan 1947, Pls XII.3, XIII.2, 7, XV.18.

6   Zoomorphic Stamp Seal   28.68

Protoliterate period *c* 3800–3000 B C. Unprovenanced.

Body carved in shape of pig or boar, half consisting of the head with expanding and transversely incised snout. Two large, unevenly spaced deep sockets between ears and snout may have been eyes or tusk sockets (original Burrell photograph shows dark inlay (?) in left socket, now missing). Perforated transversely from both sides near middle, just above base. This is flat and incised with an unusual design of five broad strokes bisected once by an axial line with irregularly placed drillings. Buff-brown *calcite* (?), chipped near base.

Height 0.017 m   Length 0.038 m

Max. diameter of bore-holes at surface 0.005 m

Unpublished.

Acquired G.F. Williams, 1953.

Occurrences of boar or pig-shaped seals such as this are widespread in Mesopotamia and Elam *c* 3000 B C (e.g. Mallowan 1947, Pl 107.9).

7   Hemispheroid Stamp Seal   28.25

Protoliterate period *c* 3300–3000 B C. Unprovenanced.

Seal of milky grey *calcite* with darker patches pierced from both ends near its maximum diameter. Convex surface polished and undecorated. Flat surface has deeply incised opposed gazelles (?) arranged in free field composition with two gazelle heads as filling ornaments. Head of smaller gazelle chipped away; long groove with curled tip extending from forehead of larger gazelle. Drill extensively used and interiors of bodies and horns roughly finished.

Height 0.015 m   Diameter 0.022 m

Max. diameter of uneven bore-holes at surface 0.006 and 0.005 m

Unpublished. Exh. Glasgow 1949, No 141.

Acquired Peter Wilson, 1948.

8   Hemispheroid Stamp Seal   28.26

Protoliterate period *c* 3300–3000 BC. Unprovenanced.

Seal of buff *calcite* with grey and red impurities, chipped at edges and pierced from both ends near maximum diameter. Areas around bore-holes rubbed concave purposely to slot into necklace (?) arrangement. Convex surface polished and undecorated. Flat, scratched surface has two roughly executed gazelles or ibexes opposed head to head, one half the size of the other. Both have small, insignificant heads and forelegs bent backwards: extensive use of drill.

Height 0.014 m   Diameter 0.024 m

Max. diameter of bore-holes at surface 0.003 m and 0.004 m

Unpublished. Exh. Glasgow 1949, No 143.

Acquired Peter Wilson, 1948.

Like the series of contemporary zoomorphic seals and pendants in the collection, stamp seals such as these occur commonly in Mesopotamia – South West Iran *c* 3000 B C at the time when, in the south, they were beginning to be replaced by cylinder seals. Animals in *tête-bêche* positions like these also belong to this last phase of the *floruit* of their production according to Amiet (1972, 48–9; *cf* Heinrich 1936, Pl 20; Mallowan 1947, Pl XIX. 12).

9 Cylinder Seal 28.17

Protoliterate period *c* 3300–3000 B C. Unprovenanced.

Squat cylinder of white stone (*dolomite*) bored from both ends. Deeply incised decoration of three antelopes in a frieze without borders. Animals unevenly spaced and in static position or with legs projecting stiffly in front as if pulling to a stop. Elongated S-curved horns, triangular heads and plump bodies; drill used for hoofs and in one instance for knees and on haunch. File (?) marks on terminals. Complete.

Height 0.018 m   Diameter 0.018 m
Diameter of bore at end 0.005 m
Unpublished. Exh. Glasgow 1949, No 131.
Acquired Sydney Moss, 1948.

Processions of animals, often executed in a more geometric, drilled style than here, were once held to be typical of the Jemdat Nasr period (Protoliterate c-d) in South Mesopotamia as well as contemporaneously in Iran (e.g. Frankfort 1939a, Pl VIIIk). It is now known however that the style co-existed with the more modelled engravings common in earlier times. This motif also had wide currency in earlier and contemporary stamp seals where the number of animals was inevitably restricted by the available space (*cf Ashmolean* Nos 82–106). It is one ideally suited to the continuous frieze afforded by the cylinder since it graphically conveys the notion of an endless procession.

10 Ram Pendant 28.22

Protoliterate period *c* 3300–3000 B C. Unprovenanced.

Couchant ram in the round. Sides very lightly incised with tucked legs and haunches; straight tail is also indicated, but most carving effort is concentrated on the head with curved horns sweeping from forehead to below the eye hollows and encircling ridged ears. Long nose and nostrils barely indicated. Cream-grey banded *calcite*; complete, with V-shaped bore-holes drilled transversely through shoulders.

Height 0.031 m   Length 0.044 m
Max. diameter of bore-holes at surface 0.003 m
Unpublished.
Acquired John Hunt, 1950.

Naturalistic models of rams or sheep such as this were found in large numbers in the 'Sammelfund' in the sacred precinct of Eanna at Uruk (Heinrich 1936, Pls 9–10). They are also well known from Susa C deposits in Elam (Le Breton 1957, 111, Fig 31.2). Contemporary North Mesopotamian animal figures tend to have their heads *regardant*. This particular example belongs to Behm-Blancke's style group IIA (1979, Pl 17).

Their frequent occurrence in the Archaic temples at Uruk together with at least one example pierced to form part of a standard (Heinrich 1936, 17) emphasizes the role of temple organisations in the integration of the religious, economic and perhaps political life of Early Sumerian communities. While often regarded as having amuletic value, the specific purpose of these figures – substitute sacrifices, votives, tallies – is not known.

11 Duck Pendant 28.19

Protoliterate period *c* 3800–3000 BC. Un-provenanced.

Duck with head resting on back, perforated through the base of its neck. Shallow eye-sockets, simple incised lines for its legs, flat, undecorated base. Complete. *Calcite*.

Height 0.022 m   Length 0.042 m

Max. diameter of perforation at surface 0.003 m

Unpublished. Exh. Glasgow 1949, No 115.

Acquired John Hunt, 1948.

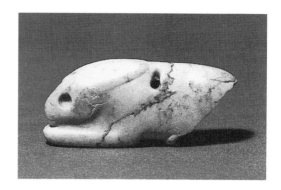

Common in larger shapes as weights starting in the late 3rd millennium BC in Mesopotamia (*cf* **55–6**) this pendant may well belong to an earlier period, when, at Tell Brak in North Mesopotamia, for example, similar duck amulet-seals occur (Mallowan 1947, Pl XI.4). They also occur in southeastern Iran in the Proto-Elamite period.

12 Hare Pendant 28.20

Protoliterate period *c* 3800–3000 BC. Un-provenanced.

Long, narrow body is shaped as *couchant* hare. Legs form flat base. Head has large eye sockets perhaps for inlays, long ears pressed down on back. Cream-coloured *calcite* with grey and brown discolouration. Worn perforation bored transversely above shoulders from both sides. Right eye and forehead chipped; rear part beyond haunches and tips of hind feet missing. Recent metal stand-peg inserted between forelegs in base.

Height 0.023 m   Length 0.055 m

Max. diameter of bore-holes at surface 0.003 m

Unpublished. Exh. Glasgow 1949, No 145.

Acquired John Hunt, 1948.

Zoomorphic pendants such as this are particularly common in Susa C (Le Breton 1957, 111, Fig 31.3) and occur more rarely at this time in Mesopotamia. See Mallowan 1947, 106–4 for survey of contemporary hare pendants in Mesopotamia and note that the Tell Brak ones are different in style or that some were worked in a different, synthetic material, namely faience.

13 Bird Pendant 28.56

Protoliterate period *c* 3800–3000 BC. Un-provenanced.

Light buff *alabaster* bird (?cock) crisply rendered with flattened body, thickened beak, incised eyes (inlays lost), concave back thinned out into undifferentiated tail feathers. Perforated from both sides at base near position of legs (not indicated). Complete.

Height 0.035 m   Length 0.039 m   Thickness 0.007 m

Max. diameter of holes at surface 0.003 m

Unpublished

Acquired G.F. Williams, 1952.

Woolley assigned a similar pendant from Ur to a period before *c* 1500 BC (1956, Pl 27.U.6473) and at Tello-Girsu they are assigned to the Jemdat Nasr (Protoliterate c-d) period, the *floruit* of the production of such animal pendants (Parrot 1948, 50, Fig 12 e–g).

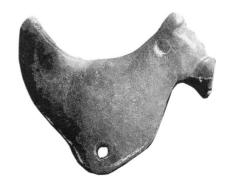

14 Bull Figurine 28.41

Protoliterate period *c* 3300–3000 BC. Unprovenanced.

Bull with accentuated haunches, straight forelegs and bent fragmentary rear legs, as if partly in kneeling position. Proficiently modelled body contrasts with poorly carved head with small, barely indicated horns (right one chipped) large, socketed eyes (for lost inlays) and circular mouth set askew. Cream-coloured *gypsum* pitted on belly and left side; slight green surface discolouration behind left foreleg; metal stand-peg recently inserted between hind legs in base.

Height 0.026 m   Length 0.049 m

Unpublished.

Acquired John Hunt, 1950.

Stone figurines of this type most commonly occur in Mesopotamia and Iran *c* 3000 BC where many achieve a liveliness and conviction hardly seen here (Le Breton 1957, 111, Figs 31, 32). Apparent wear of the head area certainly reduces its impact. Although it may have served a different purpose than the zoomorphic pendants, upright animals such as this are also found in temples.

15 Ritual Bull Vase 28.2

Protoliterate period *c* 3500–3000 BC. Unprovenanced.

Standing bull with conical, oval-rimmed vase inserted deeply into its shoulders and back (Fig 2). Deep body with incised lines of uneven depth delimiting haunches, shoulders, joints of legs and the juncture between conical vase and back. Long tail swings to adhere to left hind-leg; protruding ridge down centre of chest is horizontally incised. Small horns spring from a bar on top of the head to slightly indented ears. Two rough incisions outline the modelled eyes while a third incision indicates eyebrows. Incomplete: all four legs are broken, rim of conical vase missing, damaged muzzle. Much restoration, sometimes obscuring incised detail. Buff-cream mottled *calcite*.

Height 0.131 m   Length 0.16 m   Depth of vase 0.058 m

Max. diameter of mouth 0.05 m

McLellan Galleries, 6 top. Exh. Glasgow 1949, No 101.

Acquired Spink & Son, 1947.

2   Section of **15** showing depth of conical vessel carved into the back of the zoomorphic stand.

Form and modelling indicate that this vase was fashioned in the late 4th millennium BC when such ritual zoomorphs became popular in South Mesopotamia and Elam, in particular in Uruk Levels III-IV and Susa. That the type was used in Early Sumerian temples as part of the cultic paraphernalia is confirmed by the presence of similar goat and lion zoomorphs executed in relief on the top register of the well-known tall cult vessel from the treasure-house in the Eanna precinct in Uruk Level III/II together with a group of vessels containing gifts for the goddess Inanna (Heinrich 1936, Pls 2, 3, 38). According to a contemporary seal they were carried aloft as an offering by a man who seems to occur regularly in prominent positions on seals of the time (Fig 3).

3 Seal impression of the second half of the fourth millennium BC (*after* Moortgat 1969, Pl A.6).

These animal vases therefore were important in Early Sumerian rituals for the goddess Inanna and probably other deities as well. Depictions show that animal offerings comprised long-horned goats and lions, but other animals were also adopted for this purpose in reality (*cf.* Strommenger & Hirmer 1964, Pl 35 left), though they are not as common as might be expected. The Burrell vase therefore allows a rare correlation between Early Sumerian scenic compositions of rituals and surviving cultic paraphernalia. Unlike the large conical vessels which are heaped up with comestible produce in those scenes, nothing is shown inside these containers. Although perspectives may be deceiving, the animal vases are much smaller and so they may have contained something like precious liquids or incense. Because the cup on the back of our bull vase has an open shape, such liquids would not be meant for storage but for immediate pouring. It may well be therefore that these were intended as libation vessels or incense burners, though this one has no evidence of burning.

Some contemporary examples may have had vessels which stand proud on the backs of the animals (Moortgat 1969, Pls 15–6; Muscarella 1981a, 59.10) and this tendency to transform the animals into vessel bases prevailed subsequently. The contexts of these later ones, in one instance from the Inanna Temple at Nippur (*PK* 14, Pl 36b), indicate that they continued to serve as temple goods. The animals however have become recognizably supernatural beasts by Early Dynastic times and hence the symbolism has changed from the Early Sumerian period when the naturalistic, laden bull signified the total product of man's labours on behalf of the gods. Further diversification of this theme is asserted in the dedication of a vase in the shape of a mastiff by king Sumuel of Larsa, *c* 1894–1843 BC (Frankfort 1970, 123, Fig 137).

16 Cup With Animal Combat Support 28.45

Protoliterate period *c* 3500–3000 BC . Unprovenanced.

Small conical cup set in the centre of the upper of two tiers of animal support figures consisting of 'lion attacking bull' pairs. The upper tier rests on a solid flat rectangular base with vertically notched edges supported by the heads and manes of the lower figures. Only two of the latter survive and these have lost their legs. Upper tier: relatively small lions attack the haunches of the bulls at side of cup; another miniature rampant lion between the bulls' heads has a damaged paw resting on the shoulder of the bull to its right. Animals are *regardant* and in three-quarters relief to fully modelled. Two lions with, one without, drilled manes. Lower tier: fragmentary larger figures, the lion completely draped over the back of the bull which faces forward. There was most likely a similar pair opposite originally. The lions have distinct muzzle folds, upright rounded ears, thick manes picked out in dotted (once inlaid ?) circles executed with a drill and in the case of the lower lion, extending onto its forehead, and large, clumsily rendered forelegs with incised axial lines and five or six claws. The foreleg of the nearly complete upper bull is bent as if the animal staggers under the impact of the lion. *Ophiolite-clinochlore* with patches of dark surface discolouration; 0.005–6 m wide chisel marks on base and rough interior of lower tier.

Height 0.137 m　Length 0.128 m　Thickness 0.099 m

Unpublished.

Acquired Spink & Son, 1951.

Although not depicted in glyptic compositions, as was **15**, there can be little doubt that this ornate vessel served a similar and contemporary ritual function in Early Sumerian temples (libations/incense?). The small cup which is virtually

4　Oblique view of **16**.

concealed by the clumsy animal supports is of the same size as that on the back of the bull of **15**, material and size are similar and close parallels have also been found in temples. Thus, two-tiered examples with animals modelled in high relief on virtually identical notched platforms come from temples at Tell Agrab (Frankfort 1970, 30, Figs 17–19) and the Archaic Ishtar temple at Ashur (Andrae 1922, Pl 50a–e). The stock motif of lion attacking bull as well as stylistic peculiarities such as the incised, wide, flat lions' paws are repeated on other temple goods of the time (*cf* a spouted jug from the 'Sammelfund' at Uruk: Heinrich 1936, Pls 22, 23a). On some supports a naked hero is incorporated in a central position within the design, but here he seems to be replaced by a lion, its paw extended in exactly the same manner as that of a lion on a support from Tell Agrab (Frankfort 1970, 30, Fig 18). Ornate cult vessels such as this may have been kept as hallowed antiques in some temples, for at Tell Agrab one was recovered from a much later Early Dynastic level (*PK* 14, 184).

The detailed similarities between these elaborate supports from widely scattered temples presumably dedicated to various divinities argues for a strong unity of cultic expression and rites in early Sumer. Since these stereotyped vessels occur at the time of the advent of urban centres, they suggest that temple organisations played a significant role in the emergence of the dramatically new economic and political realities of this pristine Mesopotamian civilisation in the 4th millennium BC.

17　Sculptured Vase Fragment　28.14

Protoliterate period *c* 3500–3000 BC. Allegedly from Jemdat Nasr, South Mesopotamia.

Fragmentary, conical, flat-based vase with three bulls in relief, facing right and standing on a notched base-line just above the vessel base. Bulls' heads and forequarters are *en face*, the remaining parts foreshortened and accentuated by vertical and horizontal incisions. Traces of hooves above one bull indicate that the vessel was originally much taller with a second, upper register that probably displayed a similar procession of bulls in relief.

Chipped *limestone*.
Height 0.055 m   Diameter 0.05 m
Hannah 1953, 350.9. Exh. Glasgow 1949, No 103.
Acquired John Hunt, 1948.

18   Sculptured Vase Fragment   28.49

Protoliterate period *c* 3500–3000 BC. Unprovenanced.

Fragment of vase with high relief decoration of bull, proceeding right, *regardant*. Traces of others to either side suggest that this was originally a conical(?) vase with a procession of bulls in high relief. The preserved bull with its unnaturally foreshortened back is squeezed into a small space: the angle of the hind legs of the one in front indicates a larger space for it to stride out. The head is in bold relief, the body is carved without attempt at modelling and it has a distinctive V-incision on its haunch. *Limestone*; metal nail inserted on interior.
Height 0.085 m   Width 0.056 m
Hannah 1953, 112.4.
Acquired Spink & Son, 1952.

High relief vases with processions of bulls are typical of the Early Sumerian period in South Mesopotamia. As on impressions of the novel cylinder seals of the period (*cf.* **9**), the effect created was that of an endless frieze, an abundance of prosperity and perhaps divine forces inherent in such mighty beasts. That fertility and hence continuity and longevity was also meant to be conveyed is clear from a birthing hut incorporated in the decoration of one example from Khafaje (*PK* 14, Pl 71b). This established convention therefore was much more important than the execution and hence the finish of such vessels is often poor. Craftsmen repeated the type by rote and since the schema epitomized established order in society there was little reason for innovation. Thus the same notched base as on **16** recurs here and on other relief vessels (e.g. Muscarella 1981a, 58.9; Strommenger & Hirmer 1964, Pls 26–7). The bulls are cursorily rendered with sparing use of deep incisions to indicate musculature. In the case of the small fragment **18**, the lapidary may even have mismanaged available space since the cramped position of the preserved bull is at odds with the more extensive space allotted to the bull in front. Traces of animals above the extant register on **17** however indicate that it may have been more elaborate than normal, perhaps resembling the spouted jug from Uruk (Strommenger & Hirmer 1964, Pls 26–7) or, even more likely, a tall conical cup with two registers of bulls, rams and sheep, now in the British Museum and possibly from Uruk (Hall 1928, Pl 11.1).

It is generally thought that stone vessels with

relief sculpture of this period were reserved for temple use (e.g. Muscarella 1981a, 58–9). While this is likely to be essentially correct, it is worthwhile noting that Woolley recovered identical examples depicting a row of compressed bulls standing on a notched base from Jemdat Nasr (Protoliterate c–d) graves at Ur (Woolley 1955, Pl 31. U.18524, 20000). These funerary contexts suggest that occasionally such cultic vessels served other purposes outside the great temple organisations.

19 Stone Dish   28.8

Protoliterate period *c* 3300–3000 BC. Allegedly from Uruk (Warka, Biblical Erech), South Mesopotamia.

Flat-based dish with straight expanding sides and plain rim. White *calcite* with flaked surface and one repaired crack.

Height 0.058 m   Diameter 0.167 m

Wells 1958a, 165.12. Exh. Glasgow 1949, No 144.

Acquired Spink & Son, 1948.

20 Stone Bowl   28.48

Protoliterate period *c* 3300–3000 BC. Unprovenanced.

Deep, round-based bowl with thin, vertical sides and plain, slightly chipped rim. Blue-grey, fine-grained *igneous stone* with white flecks and rust-red spots.

Height 0.067 m   Diameter 0.108 m

Hannah 1953, 350.8.

Acquired Spink & Son, 1952.

If, as seems likely, this bowl really did originate in Mesopotamia, then on typological grounds it belongs to the Protoliterate c–d period of Sumer or its equivalent in South West Iran (Woolley 1955, Pl 66, JN30). It was during this period that stone vases became common in these regions (Le Breton 1957, 110–120, Figs 28.1, 72.1). Even the poorest graves in the 'Jemdat Nasr cemetery' at Ur, a necropolis where burials may have continued well into the Early Dynastic period, contained one or two examples.

21 Stone Jar 28.80

Protoliterate-Early Dynastic I periods
c 3300–2750 BC. Unprovenanced.
Poorly finished jar of polished, veined *alabaster*.
Disc base, globular body with sharply defined hori-
zontal shoulder and straight, inward sloping neck to
a wide, flat rim.
Height 0.117 m   Diameter 0.133 m
Unpublished.
Acquired K.G. Hewett, 1955.

This type of stone jar is commonly found in
Jemdat Nasr (Protoliterate c–d) contexts at Ur
(Woolley 1955, Pls 33 U.19401; 67.56–7) and
rather later (unless the date of the Ur material
should be lowered), in Early Dynastic I times at
sites along the Diyala River and Nippur (*PK* 14,
169.36a). It is also found more rarely during the
same periods in southwest Iran (Le Breton 1957,
110, Fig 28.24). The successors of these shouldered jars with wide brims had a special function
in later Early Dynastic periods when they appear
in ritual scenes. Thus it is supported by a goat-
stand on a votive plaque (**29**) and by a remarkable kneeling figure-stand from the Shara temple
at Tell Agrab (Moortgat 1969, Pls 55–6).

Sumerian worshipper statues   22–28

During Early Dynastic times highly ranked Sumerians began to place stone statues of themselves before the deities inside temples (Fig 5). At first these were stiffly modelled and seemingly anonymous but with their exaggerated eyes and imploring gaze, starkly effective. Later, inscriptions were sometimes incised into the shoulders or backs of the figures and a greater degree of individualism and schematized portraiture manifests itself. These inscriptions reveal that the statues were dedicated by kings, priests, grain stewards, scribes and singers, in other words the rulers and chief functionaries of the great institutions of Sumerian society. Access to the cellae of temples, the innermost rooms containing the main cult statue, was reserved for these elite groups, both male and female, and their statues, pious works as they are, may thus be interpreted as symbolizing and reinforcing the hierarchical order that prevailed in Sumer. That so many poorer quality ones were recovered from the Diyala temples suggests that in some areas statues were more readily commissioned and that greater social fluidity or at least wider direct access to the gods' houses existed.

To treat these works as lifeless entities is to misunderstand their essence. Gudea, a late 3rd millenium BC king of Lagash, had recorded about his statue: 'Statue, say to my king . . .' the 'king' referred to being the city god Ningirsu. Another of his statues was called: 'It offers prayers'. Thus they were deemed to possess a life apart from that of their dedicators and they were doubtlessly meant to represent the devotees in everlasting contact with the deity. These worshippers were depicted in standing, kneeling or seated positions; their hands clasped in front, occasionally holding an object. They wear *kannakes*, a skirt of tufted material which at times almost enveloped the whole figure. Eyes, brows and frequently the hair were inlaid or applied in bitumen, shell and other sharply contrasting materials, now usually missing. Originally they were painted. Votive worshipper statues have been found chiefly in central Mesopotamia. Regional styles and provincial work occur in outlying centres such as Susa in southwestern Iran and Tell Chuera in Syria.

5 Internal reconstruction of old Ishtar Temple cella at
   Ashur (*after* Andrae 1922, Pl 11a).

22 Worshipper Statue 28.1

Early Dynastic II Period *c* 2750–2600 B C.
Unprovenanced.

Standing figure in pleated skirt, with hands folded
below chest. Head, feet and elbows missing, some
restoration on back, chest and arms. Heavy
shoulders, angular chest, deep body; forearms joined
to top of skirt. Hands clasped, elongated fingers
together. Belt-ridge with depending incised tassel at
back of skirt which is smooth at waist, incised and
modelled pleats on lower portion. Circular dowel-
hole in base of neck, rectangular one and circular
perforation in base of skirt. *Limestone.*

Height 0.252 m   Width 0.163 m

McLellan Galleries, 5. Exh. Glasgow 1949, No 146.

Acquired Margaret Burg, 1947.

The angularity of the chest and elbows of this
statue and its rather plain skirt are typical
features of Diyala River area sculptures of the
Early Dynastic II period (*cf* Frankfort 1970, 46,
Fig 39). Although the upper torso is partly
restored, enough remains to indicate that it was
bare and hence this may be identified as a beardless male. It is not known if beards or different
types of skirts were correlated with a certain
status in society, though this seems inherently
likely. The plain, modelled pleats of the garment
are rarer than those with detailed incisions and it
has especially close analogies with skirts on
statues from the Diyala temples (Braun-
Holzinger 1977, Pls 2c, 3a, b, e, g, 6a, b). It may
thus be a northern regional variant of Sumerian
worshipper figures, though such dress fashions
were occasionally depicted elsewhere, as at Tello-Girsu (*ibid* Pl 12d).

Before the Americans began scientific excavations on the Diyala sites, a number of statues
came from the area onto the antiquities market
(Muscarella 1981A, 71) and hence it is not impossible that this is the source of our statuette.
Dowel holes here serve no ancient function and
are modern additions.

23 Worshipper Statue 28.4

Early Dynastic II period *c* 2750–2600 B C.
Unprovenanced.

Small, standing, bearded figure with disproportionately large hands clasped below chest. Head, legs
and upper arms missing. Lower parts of two hair
braids and incised, square-cut beard remain on
angular chest, so indicating a male figure. The
fingers of his hands are awkwardly modelled,
thumbs elongated. The rolled belt of his smooth
skirt has a plain tassel on his left hip and the skirt
fringe has roughly incised pleats: there are approximately three incisions to each major fold with a
triangular point. There may have been an extension
behind his legs for support; a modern (?) dowel hole
in its base. *Alabaster.*

Height 0.077 m   Width 0.047 m

Unpublished. Exh. Glasgow 1949, No 148.

Acquired Peter Wilson, 1948.

23

24

The simply incised beard and braids and the rendering of the skirt are typical of Early Dynastic II Sumerian figures, best exemplified in the group from the Abu Temple at Eshnunna (Frankfort 1970, 46 Fig 39). The hands however are larger than most comparable work, even than those in the ultra-provincial sculptures recovered from Tell Chuera in Syria (cf Moortgat 1969, Pls 70–75).

24   Worshipper Statue   28.71

Early Dynastic III period c 2600–2350 BC. Unprovenanced.

Standing clean-shaven male figure in long, flounced skirt entirely picked out in tufts with slot at back for missing belt knot. Hands are clasped at chest, arms attached near elbows to upper skirt. The large eye sockets and single line brow were once inlaid and the manner of the nose breakage is also suggestive of an inlay. There are two inscription panels: a small one on the back and a larger one over the right shoulder containing five columns, the last with the only legible signs recording the old Akkadian verb 'to dedicate'[1]. Mended and partly restored. Feet, lower back of skirt and left arm below elbow are missing. Encrusted *alabaster* (crackled/burnt?).

Height 0.367 m   Width 0.146 m

Hannah 1956, 408.16, Fig 3; Braun-Holzinger 1977, 83; Marks 1983, 26 Fig 1.

Acquired G.F. Williams, 1954.

Despite its poor condition, the figure retains much of its original quality which allows it to be compared with the best of Frankfort's Sumerian Early Dynastic III Realistic Style. The inscribed panel indicates that a notable is represented, and the fact that there are two such panels is exceptional; The one on the back may not have been inscribed. The head resembles that of the less well preserved statue of Urkisala (Frankfort 1939 b, Pls 48–9), but the robe shows further development in the treatment of the flounces and so the figure should be placed well after the start of the Early Dynastic III period. Braun-Holzinger attributes it to her Stilstufe II, broadly contemporary with Urkisala (1977, 83).

1. Translation through courtesy of E. Sollberger (pers comm 11 II 1974).

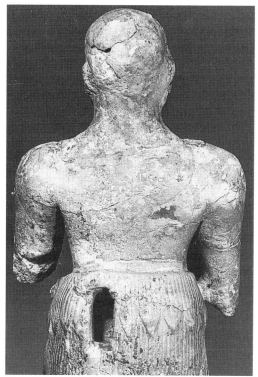

This figure is certainly more akin to work from the Diyala region than the site of Mari on the Euphrates River which has also produced many sculptures of the period. Only very rarely at the latter site do beardless figures have inscriptions and this is perhaps a telling regional difference. Thus, the figure is likely to have come from an area to the east of Mari. The neat socket where the nose should be seems more likely to have been for an inlay rather than the result of breakage, yet all known Early Dynastic III stone statues have noses modelled from the matrix material. The socket for the tassel at the back of the skirt is more convincing, though an inlay of different material would also be quite unusual.

25 Head Of Worshipper Statue 28.5

Early Dynastic III period *c* 2450–2350 BC. Unprovenanced.

Three-quarters life-sized, bald, male head with single raised eyebrow joining prominent nose. The large eye sockets have bold relief outlines. Pronounced small lower lip with a dimpled, protruding chin and modelled ears at unequal distances from the eyes. Two incisions at juncture of chin and chest indicate the neck. Back of head broken and shoulders missing. *Limestone.*

Height 0.12 m   Width 0.064 m

McLellan Galleries 7, left; Marks 1983, 27, Fig 2; Exh. Glasgow 1949, No 139; *Hayward* 42.33.

Acquired G.F. Williams, 1948.

This sensitively modelled head possesses traits that are characteristic of the late Early Dynastic III period of Sumer. Its socketed oval eyes and plain raised brows properly belong to that time (*cf* Frankfort 1939b, Pl 47.44; Strommenger & Hirmer 1964, Pls 104–5), although brows were more usually inlaid. Later, perhaps because of the preference for hard diorite, eyes are modelled, not inlaid, and there is a growing trend to incised details as on the arched eyebrows (*ibid* Pls 129–137). Its mouth is executed with thick lips, the upper sensitively pinched down at its centre, in a manner which closely associates it with sculptures from the Diyala area (e.g. Frankfort, 1939b, Pl 51 an earlier figure from Sin Temple IX; *cf* also the seated Copenhagen figure: Moortgat 1969, Pl 107). The slender pro-

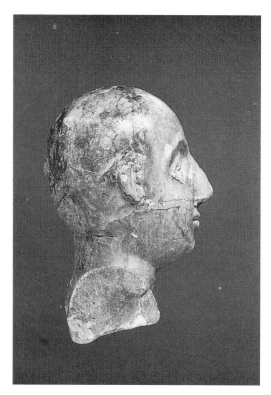

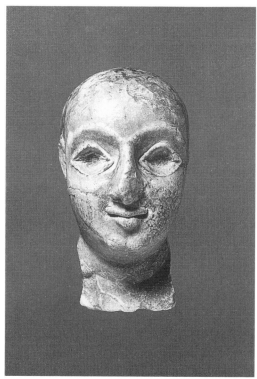

portions of the head distinguish it from these parallels as well as from the seated statue of Dudu (Moortgat 1969, Pl 103) which like the others mentioned here belong to Braun-Holzinger's Stilstufe III (1977, 62).

26 Head Of Worshipper Statue 28.11

Second half of the third millennium BC. Unprovenanced.

Only the face and part of the upper chest survive of this badly damaged statue. The left part of the forehead is sheared away and the single-line incised eye brow is slighted here. Chisel marks have not been polished smooth. Deep sockets for missing inlaid eyes. Puffy, delicately modelled lips. Dress comes up to the neck where it possesses triple ridged border and vertical incisions. *Calcite.*

Height 0.069 m   Diameter 0.038 m

Unpublished. Exh. Glasgow 1949, No 106.

Acquired John Hunt, 1949.

Although severely damaged, enough remains of the facial features and the robe to indicate that this head comes from a carefully modelled female statue, probably of the later third millennium BC. The surviving portion indicates that the dress extended right up to and round the neck covering both shoulders in the female fashion of the late third-early second millennia BC rather than draped over one shoulder as was the case for the male. It probably extended down to her calves or ankles in a series of flounces in which the individual strands are finely delineated. Coarse versions of this dress type are known at the very end of the Early Dynastic III and Akkadian periods (*cf* the relief of Enheduanna, daughter of Sargon and certain Mari figures: Moortgat 1969, Pls 95, 97, 130). Later Sumerian sculptors delighted in minute detail as on the upper part of this robe. It bears a closer resemblance to those of seated females on votive plaques (e.g. *PK* 14, Pl 117b) and freestanding sculptures of the goddesses Ningirsu and Bau (Frankfort 1970, 110, Fig 118; *PK* 14, Pl 164c) which are later products. That not all these late Sumerian statues represent deities is demonstrated by the seated figure of Enannatuma, a

priestess at the shrine of Nanna at Ur (Moortgat 1969, Pl 183).

The facial differences between these comparable figures and our fragment, including modelled rather than inlaid brows and eyes, may be due to the material. They are made from hard diorite whereas this is of much softer calcite. The few examples of calcite that survive from the late third millennium BC show that when sculptors worked in softer stone as here they followed traditional inlaying methods (*cf* Strommenger & Hirmer 1969, Pl 140).

27 Head Of Worshipper Statue 28.7

Second half of the third millennium BC. Unprovenanced.

Bald, male head with back protruding behind neck, large relief ears and narrow eyes set under a single relief line eyebrow which joins nose, now partly restored. Small mouth also restored in an elongated, slightly flabby face. Metal (?) tenon in broken base. *Calcite.*

Height 0.057 m   Width 0.04 m
Unpublished. Exh. Glasgow 1949, No 102.
Acquired G.F. Williams, 1949.

This head may have come from a statuette such as the seated figure of Dudu in the Iraq Museum, Baghdad, with which it shares its baldness, large ears and almond-shaped eyes, modelled not inlaid (Moortgat 1969, Pl 103; *cf* Strommenger & Hirmer 1964, Pls 103, 105). The eyebrows of this head however plunge more markedly to the nose, a trait seen in statuary (*ibid* Pl 133) and relief works (Moortgat 1969, Pls 195–6) belonging to the revival of Sumerian forms after the Akkadian interlude. Yet at that time brows are normally incised with fine detail, hence it is probably somewhat earlier and may belong to Braun-Holzinger's Stilstufe III (*cf* Braun-Holzinger 1977, Pls 27c, 30b). A definite attribution is not possible because of its poor preservation.

28 Head Of Worshipper Statue 28.6

Second half of third millennim BC. Un-provenanced.

Fragmentary head and neck, sheared flat on the reverse. Female with high, incised hair-braid across top of head, lightly incised eyebrows, deep sockets for inlaid eyes, now lost, long triangular nose (broken) and slightly incised mouth near weak chin. Poor workmanship noticeable especially in lack of facial modelling and simple, straight incision for mouth. White *alabaster*. Metal screw in reverse. Damaged.

Height 0.07 m   Width 0.062 m

Unpublished. Exh. Glasgow 1949, No 105.

Acquired John Hunt, 1948.

Sumerian sculptors often depicted females with elaborate coiffures in which long pigtails are swept from the nape of the neck over the crown of the head so framing the face (*cf* Frankfort 1939b, Pls 82–92; Braun-Holzinger 1977, Pls 20c, e; 21 d–f). This is most likely what the incised ridge over the forehead represents, though it is rather plain and positioned closer to the hairline than the parallels just mentioned. In Neo-Sumerian times plain, flat or rolled bands are set close to the hairline, but they are headbands rather than hair as here (*cf* Börker-Klähn 1972, 4–5, Figs 8–12).

29 Votive Plaque Fragment 28.3

Early Dynastic II period *c* 2750–2600 BC. Unprovenanced.

Fragment of top register of relief plaque with, below the top border, a beardless male figure wearing plain skirt pleated near the hem and a rampant ram with a small, high-shouldered jar between its twisted horns. The foreleg of the bearded ram rests on a sharply curved band, probably the trunk of a tree or other plant. There are shallow, parallel incisions on the body of the animal. The male has horizontally rippled hair and is shown in profile with upper torso *en face*. He is naked from the waist up, with his right fist preferred, his left arm folded back under the right. *White alabaster*, dissolved in patches on the surface. Two modern dowel holes in rough, plain reverse.

Height 0.113 m   Length 0.112 m   Thickness 0.034 m

McLellan Galleries 7 right; Exh. Glasgow 1949, No 137.

Acquired John Hunt, 1948.

Square stone plaques were frequently set up in Sumerian temples where they were dedicated by individuals to deities. They were apparently used to secure doors by means of a hook or cord passed over a knobbed peg which, inserted through a central socket preserved in virtually all

6   Conjectural reconstruction of position of **29** in top register of votive plaque.

complete plaques, held the plaque to the doorjamb (Zettler 1987, 210–14). During the Early Dynastic II and III periods they often consisted of three registers with a banquet scene in the top register and animals and other motifs in the lower two, all executed in relief (Boese 1971; Selz 1983). The standard banquet scene comprises seated figures at the opposite ends of the top register drinking beverages offered to them by servants, often accompanied by musicians or other servants. This fragment belongs to the central section of the top register of a large plaque (assuming it originally consisted of three registers) in which the cup-bearer is portrayed in such a typical stance that the scene to the right may be reconstructed with a fair degree of certainty (Fig 6). The rampant ram however is an unconventional motif in these stereotyped compositions and it merits further comment.

Animals on votive plaques are usually shown in the lower registers where they lie at rest amongst foliage (Selz 1983, Pl IV.56), are carried presumably for butchering for the feast (*ibid* Pl IX.106), are harnessed to chariots (Moortgat 1969, Pls 42–3) or are shown in combat (*ibid* Pls 46, 49). They also occur as protomes on the front of harps (*PK* 14, Pl 83), but the size of the rampant animal on this palque is much too large to belong to the sound box of such a musical instrument. The reconstruction of Fig. 6 implies that the ram formed the central motif of the top, major register of the plaque. Existing plaques with rampant animals in the top register are rare. On an example from the Inanna Temple, Level VIII at Nippur, a rearing goat is used as a filling device in an abbreviated animal combat scene at the left terminal of the register (*PK* 14, Pl 79b). There is no indication that the Burrell fragment comes from the corner of a plaque and hence the ram is placed more centrally than on the Nippur plaque. Furthermore, the band on which its forelegs rest and which passes beyond the animal requires the existence of other motifs behind the ram. Its stance and location are more closely paralleled on an otherwise unique, fragmentary plaque from the the same temple to Inanna at Nippur (Selz 1983, K.12, Pl VI). This contemporary Nippur plaque has an undeciphered inscription between the cup bearer and the seated celebrant and the whole scene is rendered in a different, and highly unusual style, but otherwise it confirms the suggested compositon of Fig 6. Yet it does not explain the role of the ram since in its place the Nippur plaque has a rampant bull in natural foliage without associated vessel as here.

Similar banquet scenes were also popular on contemporary seals and on one of these a rampant gazelle is likewise situated behind the servant (Selz 1983, Pl VIII.88). It rears in front of a separate pot stand which consists of a curved pole that supports a jar of the same shape as the one between the horns of the Burrell ram. In other seals celebrants drink with straws from such jars (Legrain 1936, Pl 42.542, 532). Selz would date the type to the end of the Early Dynastic II period (1983, Fig 6.88). The angle of the motif under the ram's hoof is so acute that it is unlikely to be a similar pot stand; and in any case, the pot is placed exactly between the ram horns here, not on a separate stand. On a seal possibly from Umma and now in Berlin a rampant caprid is shown before a deity who is seated in splendour in front of his temple. This animal supports a pot stand that consists of a table mounted on its back (Fig 7). A conical shape between its horns is probably meant to represent a vessel, very much more simplified than ours. Frankfort persuasively asserted that

this equipment was meant to be an actual stone or bronze support (1970, 45). The seal evidence therefore suggests that the rearing he-goat on the Burrell plaque is part of an elaborate vessel stand used in these ceremonies.

Unlike the caprid-shaped stand on the Berlin seal, the ram here rests its forelegs on a curved band which probably was meant to indicate another support or more likely some kind of plant trunk. The ram figures which Woolley found beside bodies 60 and 61 in the Great Death Pit at Ur (1934, Pls 71, 87–90) help to explain more fully the significance of the ram and vessel on our plaque (Fig. 8). These two remarkable rams of wood, gold, silver, lapis lazuli and bitumen from Ur have their hind legs placed on a platform and their forelegs on branches. They are often simply described as a 'goat in thicket' and less convincingly equated with the famous ram in the thicket of Genesis 23.13. Woolley himself however was at pains to emphasize that these renowned works should be regarded as applied art, as pieces of furniture (*ibid* 265). He suspected that they were supports for some perishable substance, perhaps 'a little table top on which might be stood a lamp or a pot of incense'. Such a table would have been supported by the gold-sheathed cylindrical wood uprights on the shoulders of both animals (Fig. 8). Turning to the Burrell plaque, we can see how the jar could not rest safely between the horns of the he-goat without such a support. The carver, intent on conveying the spirit of the animal, was not inclined to reveal a minor artificial detail like this and we may assume that the vessel was placed not precariously on the head of the animal between the horns as it appears to be but on a support which rose out of sight behind the head.

This plaque fragment provides graphic support for Woolley's view that the Royal Cemetery rampant he-goats were used as zoomorphic stands for small vessels. Their contexts indicate that such stands were employed in elaborate funerary rituals and so it is possible that the banquet scenes in which similar stands occur also pertain to rites for the dead. As just mentioned, there were two found together with their bearers in the Great Death Pit, PG 1237, at Ur and this may correspond with actual usage in banquets. Canonical versions of such scenes on plaques and seals have two principal figures and we may presume that each had his own vessel stand, even though it was not possible to show them on the plaques (*cf* Pritchard 1969, No 8447). Accordingly, these votive plaques may have been set up in temples as commemoratives of past heroes and the ostentatious feasts that accompanied their deaths. The Berlin seal however shows that such vessel stands also saw service in other, non-mortuary roles. No doubt the symbolism of the immensely popular banquet scenes was complex and while it is now clear that an exclusive connection with the New Year's Festival is incorrect, the recurrence of zoomorphic stands in such scenes and in sumptuous death rites suggests that there may have been more than just a fortuitous relationship.

7   Early Dynastic seal impression (*after* Moortgat 1969, Pl E. 4).

8   Goat in thicket stand from 'royal' cemetery at Ur (*from* Lloyd 1984, Pl 91).

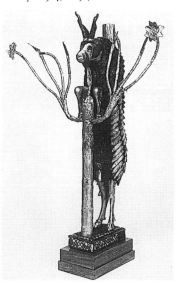

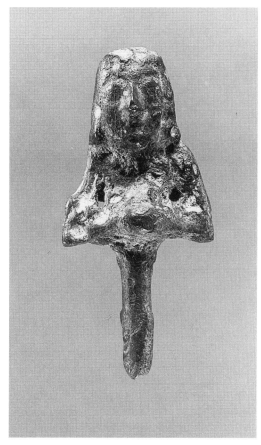

30   Foundation Figurine   28.29

Early Dynastic IIIb period *c* 2500–2350 BC.

Upper body of human figure with hands folded at chest; below this the body is in the shape of a tenon, remaining length 0.03 m. Shoulder-length hair is horizontally rippled, large eyes are slightly incised. Large nose, small mouth, protruding elbows. Most details are lost because of corrosion. Cast *copper*.

Height 0.07 m   Width 0.034 m
Unpublished.
Acquired G.F. Williams, 1950.

This type of figurine was used as a foundation deposit in Sumer for a limited period in the middle of the third millennium BC. It is amongst the first of a series of types that persisted for the entirety of ancient Mesopotamian civilisation (Rashid 1971, 660 Table 1). Extant examples appear to be of copper (Van Buren, 1931, 6–10). Some pegs were inscribed and in general they suggest that originally the peg on this one was longer. Nevertheless, the figure is still smaller in size than the examples of the time of Entemena, King of Lagash, and it lacks the horns and beard of his time. While ante-dating the close of this particular type of peg figure therefore, it does not come at the very beginning since it lacks the abstraction of the torso seen on the earliest (*ibid* Fig 2). Apart from those obtained through purchase and one example from Bismaya, all early stratified figurines were found at Tello-Girsu.

Foundation figures were typically deposited in or below the walls of temples in order to protect these sacred dwellings of the gods from evil forces (Ellis 1968). They commemorate the establishment of the temple and the role of the ruler in its foundation. (see also **40**).

31 Bearded Head Fitting 28.15

Early Dynastic III period *c* 2600–2350 BC. Unprovenanced.
Head with large eye sockets, their inlays now lost, single line incised eyebrow, incised parallel lines for hair. Remaining sides of head framed by long, full beard curled at the tips of its strands. Mouth and nose are effaced. Socketed and perforated on reverse. *Calcite(?)* with some red discolouration.
Height 0.053 m   Width 0.041 m
Unpublished. Exh. Glasgow 1949, No 116.
Acquired Winifred Williams, 1949.

This head could represent the Sumerian 'hero' who is frequently shown in combat with lions, or a supernatural animal of the type which sport such flamboyant beards. It is not from a bearded bull's head, the animal most commonly supplied with these elaborate beards (*cf* Woolley 1939, Pls 142, 212), since there are no traces of the animal's horns or sockets for them. Bearded creatures such as this often figure in divine or mythological scenes and so it closely reflects the Sumerian world of the fantastic.

The complex tenon on the reverse, which was pierced transversely to receive a wire or rivet for fastening the object, suggests that it was a furniture fitting or the like.

32 Bull Inlay 28.66

Early Dynastic II–III period *c* 2750–2350 BC. Unprovenanced.
Bearded bull proceeding left and modelled on one side only in high relief, with background stone remaining between the fore and hind legs and tail. Sensitively modelled with high, bony haunch, small fetlock, squared beard, and large ear set well behind horns which sweep forward. Unpolished, flat reverse shows narrow gauge chisel marks and, behind its head, an irregular protrusion to serve as a tenon (?). Hind legs, horn tips and beard broken. Cream coloured *alabaster.*
Height 0.07 m   Length 0.094 m   Thickness 0.023 m
Unpublished.
Acquired G.F. Williams, 1953.

A Sumerian source for this bull figure is indicated by its general heavy style and the addition of a beard. The significance of such beard attachments is much debated particularly with respect to Sumerian ideas of interaction between the natural and spiritual worlds. With the possible exception of some compositions from Uruk, deities were not represented in human guise until occasionally in the Early Dynastic period. Then and later, when they become much more common, the iconographical detail conventionally used to signal their identity is a set of bull's horns. Prior to that time, and indeed contemporaneously, transcendent powers and perhaps even specific deities, were associated with images such as this bearded bull. At a general level, the startling vision of a bearded bull was presumably meant to convey the presence of the supernatural, combined with ideas of fertility and strength.

Small scale figures were undoubtedly inlaid into all manner of furniture and architectural works in Sumer. One frieze from the facade of the temple of Ninkhursanga at al Ubaid has a milking scene in which white limestone and shell figures are inlaid into a bitumen background (Strommenger & Hirmer 1964, Pl 78). The height of the larger cows is much the same as this so its small size does not militate against its use in an architectural setting. There are a number of stylistic differences — the legs of the Ubaid animals in the milking scenes are individually rendered for example, even though other limestone inlays are treated as ours (Hall & Woolley 1927, Pl 37.T.O. 306) — and, since the Ubaid bulls are naturalistically rendered without beards, the subject matter for the Burrell figure would have been more demonic and more overtly supernatural. Mythological inlay animals were found in a more scattered state at Ubaid (Hall & Woolley 1927, 88) and an almost identical example, dated too early by Contenau, is in the Louvre (1947, 1987, Fig. 1076).

At Ubaid, Woolley noted that the solid backgrounds of certain limestone figures were painted black and that normally they were more poorly carved than the shell inlays because they were once painted overall (Hall & Woolley 1927, 88–90). No trace of paint survives here and musculature is sensitively modelled. Woolley did not mention the existence of tenons on the reverse of the Ubaid inlays and hence this example with its clear protrusion may have come from a different setting.

33

33 Bull's Head 28.36
Late fourth-early third millenium BC.
Unprovenanced.

Bull's head in the round, broken at neck from a
larger object. Its muzzle is set slightly askew,
massive horns curl forward along the head, their
tips touching, projecting ears behind the horns are
broken and large oval eyes with single incised
outline are set below the horns. Chipped yellowish
limestone with modern screw-hole at base of neck.

Length 0.04 m   Height 0.04 m

Hannah 1953, 112.2.

Acquired Spink & Son, 1951.

Bulls' heads with massive, curled horns like these
are common in late 4th-2nd millennium Sumer.
It is akin to the heads of bulls on vases like **15** of
the Protoliterate period and although the horns
here are much larger, similar ones do occur on
sculpture of the late 4th millennium BC
(Moortgat 1969, Pls 15, 16). The absence of twist
in the neck indicates that the figure does not
belong to the common relief vessels and
recumbent animals with heads *regardant*. Later
renderings of bull's heads, at least from the Early
Dynastic III period, tend to elaborate the brows
around the eyes and to have projecting horns (*cf*
Woolley 1934, Pls 114–17, 119–20, 125 top), so
it may have come from an earlier figure in all
probability from Sumer.

34 Bovid Amulet 28.24

Early Dynastic III period *c* 2600–2350 BC.
Unprovenanced.

Standing cow facing left and superficially modelled
on one side only, but with two eye sockets. Musculature, ears and horns barely indicated in this in-
tractible *shell* material. Overlarge eye sockets have
lost their inlays. No indication of tail. Dull brown
white surface discolouration on obverse, cream-
coloured on reverse. Pierced transversely just below
middle of back.

Height 0.028 m   Length 0.042 m   Thickness
0.006 m

Unpublished.

Acquired John Hunt, 1950.

Animal pendants or amulets made of shell in
Sumer and surrounding areas are normally
depicted in a recumbent posture for conventional and practical reasons, the latter to
prevent the legs breaking (*cf* Curtis 1982, Pl 4b).
Upright examples from Ur include a bovid
(Woolley 1955, Pl 27, U.14407) and a bearded
goat in metal (Woolley 1934, Pl 142, U12469).
Our example is so worn and flat that it might be
regarded as an inlay from a frieze of the kind
known to include cattle, like that from the Early
Dynastic Temple to Ninkhursanga at al Ubaid
(see **32**), were it not for traces of an eye on the

reverse and its small size. The head was modelled partly in the round therefore and so it may have projected forward from a piece of furniture to which it was secured by means of a stud originally inserted through the perforation. That this rather untidy method of fixing inlays was occasionally used in Mesopotamia is indicated by a similar dowel hole though the body of a small shell duck or goose figure from Mari (Parrot 1954b, 166, Pl XIX.2) and an unprovenanced bull 'amulet' (*Glyptique* No. 548).

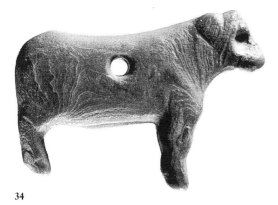

34

35 Bull's Head Terminal 28.23

Late 4th–3rd millennium B C. Unprovenanced.

Cylindrical object with bull's head terminal, the opposing end broken at a vertical perforation. The miniature bull's head is sensitively treated with wrinkles on the bridge of its nose and deep eye sockets for missing inlays; ears are set behind the relatively massive horns which curl from a central bar on to the forehead. Two slighter incisions extend backwards and downwards from the eyes, to meet in one instance a single, in the other a double line delimiting the jaws. Light red *limestone*.
Height 0.015 m Length 0.043 m
Unpublished.

Acquired Peter Wilson, 1948.

The use of inlays for eyes, the treatment of the horns and the rounded ears of the bull are Sumerian stylistic traits. Woolley obtained an identical fragmentary example, probably on the antiquities market, during his work in South Iraq (B.M. 118023). Its date and use are also unknown. In adjacent Iran, many small objects were enriched with animal-head terminals, sometimes executed in precious metals (*cf* Amiet 1966, 422, Pl 320), but the style of this head is at home in Mesopotamia. There pins, for example, occasionally have zoomorphic terminals and while gazelle-headed bone ones from Nuzi are perforated in the same way as ours (Starr 1937, Pl 127. T, U, U_2), they obviously served a different function from this much heavier object. Zoomorphic terminals are known from figural art to have decorated furniture and smaller objects such as fly-whisks (e.g. Hrouda 1965, Pls 16.1–14; 32.19–20). Whetstones, like that belonging to King Tukulti-Mer of the 11th century B C, were also capped by animal heads, but these are of metal (Braun-Holzinger 1984, Pl 71. 378–9), probably like the terminals on late furniture.

Sumerian love of embellishment is well attested and animal protomes, such as those on Queen Pu-abi's 'sledge-chariot' (Woolley 1934, Pl 122), are one manifestation of this penchant. Stone fixtures on furniture are probably attested by a somewhat larger human-headed bull from the Nintu temple at Khafaje which Frankfort interpreted as belonging to the armrest of a throne (1970, 59, Fig 61) and a bull's head protome from the palace at Mari (Parrot 1959, Pl 74.2274). On both these and on a Susa D lion protome (LeBreton 1957, 121, Fig 44.1, 2) the perforation is bored horizontally through the tenon, and so the vertical arrangement of the Burrell bar suggests that it may have been secured to a different element of furniture.

Evidence for an alternative use as a pendant is provided by an unusual perforated bar, some 8 cms in length, with bull's head at one end and an axe blade at the opposite terminal. Although the cylindrical projection behind the head of our fragment would have to expand markedly to form such a blade, its original shape was probably akin to this object. It is interpreted as a votive axe pendant of the Ur III period and is unprovenanced (*Glyptique* No 587).

35

36 Fish Amulet 28.67

Sumerian? Unprovenanced.

The fish is modelled and incised on one side only of this *shell* with mother-of-pearl iridescence. Lower body between a thin, rectangular tenon and the missing tail is cross-hatched with incisions; upper part is worn. Large eye socket retains traces of bitumen for the eye inlay (lost); mouth distorted through breakage.

Height 0.025 m   Length 0.053 m   Thickness 0.009 m

Unpublished.

Acquired G.F. Williams, 1953.

Fish was one of the major animal species sacrificed to the gods of Sumer and Akkad and vast quantities of their bones have been found in Protoliterate temples at Eridu, Uruk and Tello-Girsu (Van Buren 1948). It was a motif commonly employed for pendants made of precious materials (Woolley 1934, Pl 142; *Glyptique* No 549) and shell (Heinrich 1936, Pl 131; Parrot 1956, Pl LX.201, 244, 271, 370). It figured in scenes on votive plaques (*PK* 14, Pl 79b), cylinder seals, and statues (Strommenger & Hirmer 1964, Pl 162). Bread or pastry was even moulded in the shape of fish (Parrot 1959, Pls XVI, XXI).

The shell fish amulets just mentioned are provided with holes for suspension. Unless such existed on a missing part of this object, it may have served a different function, conceivably as an inlay, a reconstruction which would explain why it was worked on one side only. Shell was a favoured medium for inlay friezes and panels on the sound boxes of musical instruments and the like in Sumer and in Syria. The fact that this object is fashioned in relief however suggests that, if it was an inlay, it may have belonged to an architectural frieze since only they have relief inlays.

On the other hand, it is rather small for display in such a setting and our knowledge of the techniques used to decorate portable goods is by no means complete.

37 Socketed Axehead 28.16

Early Dynastic III period *c* 2600–2350 BC. Allegedly from 'Tall Lagash' (= Tello, ancient Girsu).

Lobate bladed axehead with blade set at an acute angle to the slightly tapered, socketed shaft. Moulded shaft base, flat relief collar extending along blade at its top. Scratched black surface, mottled green. *Chlorite* (with cronstedtite). Fig 9.

Height 0.081 m   Length 0.15 m   Diameter of shaft socket 0.015/0.017 m

Unpublished. Exh. Glasgow 1949, No 104.

Acquired John Hunt, 1948.

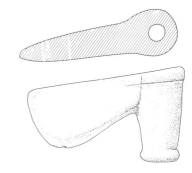

9   Socketed axehead **37**.

This axehead is made of such a soft stone, comparable to steatite, that it must have served as a model rather than a functional weapon. In spite of surface scratches, it shows little signs of wear and its lobate blade is very blunt. It is in fact an imitation of a rather specific type of metal weapon. Socketed bronze axeheads with features approximating to this copy occur especially in Iran and Mesopotamia during the mid-late third millennium BC (Deshayes 1960, 156–8, Pl XIX.1–2). These are characterized by lobate blades set at acute angles to the shaft which has strap and rounded mouldings at its terminals. There are minor modifications and Mesopotamian examples usually have obliquely cut-away shaft bases unlike ours with its flat cut base. This feature is noticeable on extant examples from the 'Royal' cemetery at Ur (Woolley 1934, Pl 237) and on representations of the period which document the prestigious nature of the weapon in question. Thus, heavily armed warriors carved in shell on a panel from Mari (Fig 10) and inlaid into the top register of the war side of the 'Royal Standard of Ur' (Strommenger & Hirmer

10   Shell inlay warrior from Mari (*after* Calmeyer 1969, 10, Fig 4).

1964, Pl XI) carry these, as do massed infantry on Eannatum's 'Stele of the Vultures' where the distinctive upper strengthening mouldings of the axeheads are also visible (*ibid* Pl 66). The length of its missing handle may be judged from one found relatively intact at Ur which measured 47 cm (Woolley 1934, Pl 153). The socket for the handle is quite large in metal axes, as one would expect of a functional weapon, hence the small diameter of our socket further corroborates its non-functional role.

Within the area of the distribution of comparable bronze axeheads, moulded flat cut bases seem to occur more often in Elam (Tallon 1987, vol 1, 73–4; vol 2, 139–140.21–7) and hence this imitation may be based on an Iranian regional variant. Sources of chlorite are well known in Iran, but since it was imported together with steatite in large quantities into Mesopotamia in the Early Dynastic III – Akkadian periods, the material is not a secure guide to place of manufacture or use of our copy.

That this model was not an effective weapon is clear, but since it is virtually unique and models of weapons are rare in Mesopotamia and Iran, its use is by no means obvious. Early models of tools or weapons are known sporadically at least from the Ubaid period when they appear in pottery (Woolley 1955, Pl 16, U.14993; L.BM 56.9–8–136; U.16221, presumably with a broken blade, is roughly analogous to the Burrell type and should perhaps be dated to the later 3rd millennium; *cf Brussels* 66.6). Pottery seems to be the usual medium for early imitations and Amiet has suggested that those belonging to the late 3rd-early and 2nd millennium BC served as votives, or as tokens to be used in transactions (1986, 156–7). Inscriptional evidence and contexts indicate that during the 2nd – 1st millennium BC copies of different materials were offered as votives. A Kassite stone axe that bears a dedicatory inscription to Marduk mentions the donor, Adad-ušabši, and even the type of stone (Sheil 1917, 91). Choice of material was obviously significant. In very rare cases belonging to Kassite Babylonian kings, from Kurigalzu II (1332–1308 BC) through most of the following century, axes were modelled in blue glass, probably coloured in imitation of precious lapis lazuli. Peters reasonably described these as votives (1898, 160, 374) and the royal inscriptions on them indicate that they were dedicated to the gods Enlil and Ninurta (Brinkman 1976, 188, 224–5, 263–4, 488–9). Granite pick and hammer blades, presumably ceremonial or votive in nature, were embedded in the great E-Nun-Maḫ at Ur (Woolley 1974, 50–1).

Others belong to earlier periods. A fragmentary greenstone example from Old Babylonian levels at Nippur carries an inscription 'Property of Nin[. . .]' (Gibson 1975, 44–5, Fig 28.3a–b). It was probably dedicated to a goddess. If we leave aside the couchant lion that adorns its shaft, the basic shape of this axe is similar to ours. More significant still is the recent publication of a chlorite shaft hole axe from Level IVB at the chlorite producing site of Tepe Yahya in Iran since it clearly demonstrates that carvers there executed model weapons in this soft material. It is decorated with an incised bird (Lamberg-Karlovsky 1988, 76, Fig 2 G).

Model axes continued to be offered in the 1st millennium BC. This is evident for example from the context of a miniature axe model found in the temple at Surkh Dum (Muscarella 1988 b, 135).

The examples of Mesopotamian axe imitations demonstrate the prevalence of the votive nature of models, the decided preference for rare stones and the high status of donors. Although most votive offerings just mentioned belong to the second millennium BC, others were certainly placed in temples during earlier periods in Sumer and Elam. At that time, the practice of duplicating in steatite/chlorite cultic paraphernalia made of metal is well attested, for example in the case of Gudea's libation beakers (see 87). The rarity of 3rd millennium BC chlorite axeheads therefore is all the more striking and although they were most likely used as votives, we cannot exclude other uses. If Woolley is correct and the Ur non-functional weapons served as parade items (1934, 301) — a strictly funerary role may also be considered — then we may discount this stone example as one used in military ceremonies since the Ur examples are all of precious metals. Mother of pearl was another material used for an imitation weapon in the Ur cemetery (*ibid* Pl 101). Weapons occasionally appear as emblems in the world of the super-

natural on seals of the period (*cf* Fig 25), and so another arena in which it may have found service is as part of a cult statue for example.

38   Cylindrical Stand(?)   28.12

Near Eastern *c* 2600–2000 BC(?). Unprovenanced.

Sub-circular, flat-based support with tapered sides carved with contiguous vertical engaged 'columns', each lightly incised with lozenges. A horizontal incision occurs mid-height on the exterior, while the interior has larger, plain attached 'columns'. In the rim are four, circular, deep sockets and the internal surface of the base is depressed. Rough incisions on the flat 'rim'. Green-black, fairly soft altered coarse *gabbro*.

Height 0.049 m   Diameter 0.075 m

Unpublished. Exh. Glasgow 1949, No 147.

Acquired G.F. Williams, 1949.

The soft stone steatite or chlorite, to which this coarse gabbro may be compared, was used for vessels in North Syria (Muscarella 1981a, 232–3), Mesopotamia and areas further to the east at different times in antiquity. The cylindrical shape of the object is similar to vessels of the first of two major phases of popularity in eastern regions (*cf* Amiet 1986, 124). During the 3rd millennium BC there emerged in Iran, the Gulf and Mesopotamia an unprecedented production and distribution of these carved steatite/chlorite vessels. Since they have been found as far apart as Mari on the Euphrates River and sites in the Indus Valley and since sources and production are centred on the southern Iranian Plateau at locations such as Tepe Yahya and Shahdad, the purpose and mechanics of this long distance trade have been the subject of lively debate. The significance of much of the decoration is also elusive. Most examples from Iran and Mesopotamia are adorned with representational motifs such as scorpions and date palms, and geometric designs such as guilloches, whirls and mat patterns. Some of the most elaborate are 'hut pots' which seem to portray architectural facades. It is the engaged columns on the exterior of the Burrell object (*cf* de Miroschedji 1973, Pls IV–V) as well as its morphology which link it to this series of buckets.

That stated however, the affinities are only of the most general kind. Buckets have thin walls and rims, smooth-surfaced interiors and low relief decoration. This has a thick wall incorporating deep rim sockets, unfinished interior and coarse relief decoration (Fig 11), features that distinguish it from other vessel types also (*cf* Woolley 1955, Pl 35). In spite of its suggestive shape therefore it does not appear to have served as a vessel. The rim sockets are deep and hence structural rather than mere slots for incrustations as in cylindrical vessels of bitumen from early 2nd millennium BC Susa (*cf* Amiet 1966, 278, Fig 208). Presumably the rough interior was not meant to be seen and so something was permanently fixed on to the cylinder. It may therefore have served as a stand or support. Its closest analogy comes from Tepe Yahya Level IV A. This is described as an 'ink well' and although it has a square shape and lacks sockets, it has similar thick walls, circular depression and rough architectural decoration (Lamberg-Karlovsky 1988, 76, Fig 21).

The Tepe Yahya 'ink well' has what may be interpreted as incised niches and a stylized hut on its walls, the Burrell support has engaged columns. Both recall South Mesopotamian architectural features. Thus the cross-hatches on the columns resemble the manner in which bundles of reeds were tied in the construction of buildings in South Mesopotamia (*cf* Woolley 1955, 8, Fig 3) or the schematic depiction of imbrications on palm trunks. The latter were imitated in attached brick half columns on the entrance of the monumental bastion of King Warad-Sin (1834–1823 BC) at Ur (Woolley 1939, 42, Pls 29b, 30b) and other Mesopotamian sites. Simplified models of such engaged columns occasionally served as stands (*cf* Contenau 1941, 52–3). Niches are characteristic of important buildings in Mesopotamia and Elam. Thus the architectural decoration, as well as the morphology of both objects, point to their association with hut pots of the intercultural style. Given the rarity of the type, it is possible that the ultimate origin of the Burrell stand is from the region of Tepe Yahya.

11 Cylindrical stand 38.

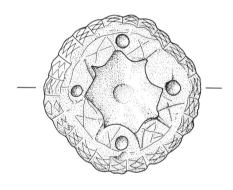

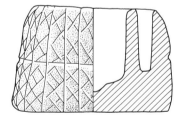

39 Seated Goddess Holding Child 28.10

Ur III period *c* 2112–2004 BC. Unprovenanced.

Seated goddess holding a cylindrical object, probably a cup, in her right hand and in the other a child with its left arm along its waist, its right extended to the cup. The divine crown consists of a pair of horns sweeping forward from a large, rectangular hairbun at the back of the head. Expressively large facial features with plain ridged eyebrows, modelled eyes and slightly twisted mouth. The robe is drawn over the left shoulder only and it is pleated at the waist and hem, the latter with fine undulating lines. The hem conceals feet as it nearly touches the flat base. Straight-sided concave-seated throne, doubly recessed on the two remaining sides. Modern dowel hole in base. Blackened and flaked *alabaster*.

Height 0.103 m   Width 0.036 m

Unpublished. Exh. Glasgow 1949, No 136.

Acquired G.F. Williams, 1949.

Statuettes of enthroned goddesses appear in Mesopotamia at least by the late 3rd millennium BC (Woolley 1976, Pls 54, 55a). The identification of earlier examples of seated females as deities is disputed (Spycket 1981, 173–4). While most females are dressed with flounced robes drawn over both shoulders (e.g. Woolley 1976, Pls 54–5), examples with the right shoulder free are also well known (Strommenger & Hirmer 1969, Pl 128 above right; Spycket 1981, Pl 139). On a Late Akkadian seal that belonged to a wet nurse named Daguna, a female wears a similar plain fringed, off-the-shoulder robe (Muscarella 1981a, 89, Pl 46). Another chronological indicator is provided by the remarkably large hairbun on our figure. These were fashionable on female terracottas at Susa where such figures occur in levels of the Ur III and the early second millennium BC (Spycket, pers comm 22.8.1988).

Other features of this statuette are more unusual and they raise questions concerning its state of completion and authenticity. Thus the facial features of both goddess and child are rather coarse and they seem unfinished. The cubical throne is a variant of normal types which are plain, inscribed or decorated with birds, vessels and furniture elements (Woolley 1976, Pls 54–5; Spycket 1981, 172–3, Pls 117, 179). This has architecturally recessed sides like those on altars (Woolley 1976, Pls 44–5). Extant thrones for statuettes however are not sculpted in the same manner as altars. Yet this discrepancy should not be regarded as sufficient to discount our statuette since contemporary terracottas (Woolley 1976, Pls 80.144, 81.152) and later *kudurru*, or boundary stones, bear thrones with such recessed panels (King 1912, Pl 77). There are also minor features, like the entirely concealed feet, which are unusual.

Most striking in this medium is the novelty of the composition of goddess with child. In his survey of representatives of nursing females, Kühne (1978) corrects the prevalent impression thay they were extremely rare in Western Asia, but he is unable to quote a stone example in the round. The standing goddesses(?) with children on a Tell Chuera stele of the mid-third millennium BC are of a different style and executed in relief. Ours is a seated, clothed version of a type that became relatively common in terracotta in South Mesopotamia in the late third — early second millennium BC. Usually the child is shown in the act of suckling (Barrelet 1968, Nos 528–30, 592–5; Amiet 1966, Pl 121). There are a few however in which the child is depicted *regardant* as here.

In two notable instances the child is seated and it has a disproportionately large and crudely rendered head. One comes from the Archaic Temple of Ishtar at Ashur (Andrae 1922, Pl 57 ak) and there the female lays her hand on the head of the child. Kühne would date it to the early 2nd millennium BC (1978, 508). The large size of the child's head is particularly evident on the second example, a late 3rd millennium BC terracotta from Ur (Woolley 1925, Pl VIII.2.7). It would seem therefore that it was the norm to render older, weaning children in this seated posture and with enlarged heads. The unusual proferred cup in the Burrell sculpture becomes explicable in this context as a receptacle for alternative forms of feeding.

The terracottas support the argument that the Burrell statuette is genuine and in a finished state. It is a unique representation in stone of a type more commonly known in terracotta, and it is a significant addition to an uncommon theme in Western Asia. The seated goddess is probably to be identified with Ninkhursanga who is referred to in Bablylonian texts as 'mother of all children' or Nintu who carries on her head a turban and 'a bull's horn' (Kühne 1978, 512).

40 Foundation Figurine 28.75

Ur III period *c* 2112–2004 BC. Allegedly from Uruk, South Mesopotamia.

Standard nail figure carrying compressed biconical basket on head. Beardless male with accentuated eyes, indented chin and arms raised to basket which rests on a notched ring. The figure is naked from the waist up. Largely effaced inscription on plain skirt; no indication of legs or feet. Cast arsenical *copper*.

Height 0.27 m   Width 0.09 m

Wells 1958a, 164.4; *Hayward* 42.332.

Acquired Spink & Son, 1955.

This is a later example of the anthropomorphic foundation figures introduced above (see **30**). It belongs to a canephore type that first appeared in the reign of Gudea of Lagash in the post-Akkadian period and then became especially common during the Ur III – Isin/Larsa periods (*c* 2112–1763 BC). Many more examples of the Ur III period are known due to the active royal building programmes of this bureaucratic dynasty (Rashid 1971, 660 Table 1). In the ceremonies that initiated constructions, figures were placed in brick boxes together with a tablet that repeated the text inscribed on the figure's robe. As is evident from *in situ* examples, mainly from Nippur and Susa, this assemblage was usually deposited at the sides of gateways or at the corners of temples, in other words at critical points under monumental, public structures. The box was water-proofed inside with a bitumen lining and the figure was wrapped in cloth (Hansen 1970, 14 n.25). On the head of all these figures is the basket of earth which the king carried to the construction site as part of the building rites. Since kings were regarded as the servants of the gods and the construction of a dwelling for a deity was ostensibly carried out at the deity's command, sacred rituals naturally attended such an enterprise. Carrying the head basket was a rite that was depicted at least from the time of Ur-Nanshe of Lagash in the mid-third millennium BC.

The workmanhsip of this worn figure is rather more awkward than that usually expended on those of the great builder King Ur-Nammu (2112–2095 BC) and it may therefore represent a later ruler, perhaps his successor Shulgi

(2094–2047 BC). His figures, however, usually have more developed pectorals. Unfortunately, the inscription which would normally supply the name of the king is illegible. Foundation figures of Shulgi's time have been found at Nippur, Susa and in the Eanna at Uruk (Ellis 1968, 64).

Sixteen foundation figures of Shulgi from temples at Susa are of > 96.7% copper (Tallon 1987, vol 1, 308–9; vol 2, 341–3.1321–1336; *cf* Schlossman 1976, 21). They do not match other copper-based metals from that city. One way to account for this discrepancy is to suggest that foundation figures came from a central workshop, from whence they were distributed to monumental works inaugurated by royal decree, and taken in the entourage of the king when he went to initiate the construction himself. That centre would probably be located at the capital, Ur, but analysis of a Mesopotamian example shows that it is an alloy with 93.5% copper (Moorey 1985, 60–1; Muscarella 1988b, 305–13). Either different mechanisms of production and distribution existed or alloying practices changed in the course of time. Our analyses (Appendices A and B) do not enable us to chose between the two groups.

41 Head Of Deity   28.53

Ur III/Isin-Larsa period *c* 2112–1763 BC. Unprovenanced.

Head with single pair of horns, traces of wavy hair and curls above relief brows meeting a short nose. Small eyes modelled without pupils, large mouth and no ears. Broken surface at back of head has a calcium incrustation. Fragment of figurine. Buff slipped red *terracotta*.

Height 0.041 m   Width 0.052 m
Hannah 1953, 112.7.
Acquired John Hunt, 1951.

Three terracotta heads of this rare type from Tello-Girsu are attributed by Marie-Thérèse Barrelet to the late 3rd-early 2nd millennium BC (1968, 163–4, Pl VIII.79–81). She found no suitable parallels and so the attitude of the complete figurine is not known. They all bear horns of divinity and the Burrell head compares well with Barrelet 80 which is better preserved. During this period in Sumer there was a tremendous vogue for mass-produced terracotta plaques and figurines with religious themes. They were common in the houses and chapels at Ur when private family life became stronger and deceased members were buried below a floor of the house rather than in a cemetery, as was customary earlier. This terracotta therefore represents a more private trend in the development of Mesopotamian religion. The rather worn appearance of its facial details may be due to production from an old mould in which individual features had become smooth through use.

42　Lion Head　28.37

Isin-Larsa/Old Babylonian period *c* 2000–1600 BC. Unprovenanced.

Head of lion with stylized mane, broken away from larger sculpture. Forcefully modelled and incised head with wide open jaws, long flared nose incised transversely and bordered by single ridges, whiskers indicated schematically by loops and protruding eyes and ears finished with notched rims. Six bosses above the eyes, beside the ears and on the cheeks are impressed with dot rosettes. The rounded ears are pieced through to the smooth, concave interior and four tassel-like appendages depend from the ears over the cheeks. The mane falling over its chest consists of converging incised ribs divided by a slight horizontal incision and edged by a border with incised zigzag. On the remaining stubs of the sides are arched relief bands with incisions and beyond the upright band of hair between the ears traces of relief patterns. Traces of red paint in the eyes and mouth. Incisor teeth are broken; extensively restored, greenish-white *terracotta*.

Height 0.535 m　Width 0.425 m

Marks 1983, 28, Fig 53; *Hayward* No 333.

Acquired John Hunt, 1950.

Large-scale sculptural works in terracotta became popular in Sumer and Elam in the first half of the second millennium BC (e.g. Muscarella 1981a, 112–13, 194–5; Hrouda 1977, Pl 8). Amongst the most imposing works are guardian lions set at the entrances to temples like that of Nisaba at Tell Harmel, ancient Shaduppum near Baghdad (Fig 12). These were near life-size representations generally meant to convey the 'terror of the gods' according to an inscription of the time of Gudea who installed lions in gates at Tello-Girsu (Spycket 1981, 222).

They may also have been more directly associated with specific deities. Depictions of several with fully elaborated manes occur on contemporary terracotta plaques where, together with other guardian figures, they flank deities (e.g. Dalley 1984, 185, Fig 57). Two are carved on the throne for the statue of the goddess Inana/Narundi which the *en*, or governor, of Susa had placed in a temple (Amiet 1966, Fig 166). The details of their manes are similar to those on the Burrell head and the bolt upright seated posture is the same as that of the Tell Harmel lions. We

12　Guardian lions in a temple at Shaduppum (Tell Harmel) in south Mesopotamia (*from* Strommenger & Hirmer 1964, Pl 156).

Mesopotamia · 65

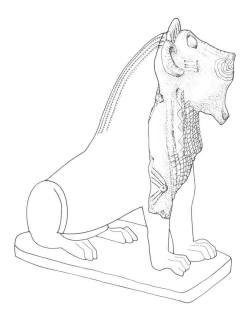

13 Conjectural reconstruction of lion 42.

an external guardian figure rather than one situated beside a cult statue.

Some two dozen complete and fragmentary examples are known and their emphatic concentration in South Mesopotamia points to that region as the ultimate source of the Burrell lion. Six examples guarded the temple at Tell Harmel, two were found at Khafaje Tell D (no details save heights of 2–3 feet), approximately six at Tello-Girsu, seven at Susa, one each at Isin, Tell Usiyeh and Nasirya (Spycket 1988; Muscarella 1981a, 195 with references; *Iraq* 45, 1983, 223). Many are incompletely published, but it is clear that several come from temples and that they too were painted in red and black. Other examples of this period were made in stone and bronze (Spycket 1981, 289, n.291, 290–1).

So similar is the Burrell lion to two others put up for sale at l'Hôtel Drouot in Paris in 1947 that they once probably constituted part of a set in a Babylonian temple. Parrot published the two when he purchased them for the Louvre (1954a); a third head offered in the same lot, it is argued here, was acquired by Sir William Burrell in 1950.

The three heads were all roughly detached from their bodies, presumably to facilitate transport (Fig 14a–c). The Louvre lions (Fig 14b, c) have similar schematized features and they also rely for effect on gaping jaws and exaggerated, incised details. Thus their manes are comprised of panels of parallel slashed ribs, hair on the forehead is rendered by vertical cylinders of clay,

may thus confidently infer from its close stylistic similarities with the latter that the Burrell head was once part of a lion in the *sejant rampant* attitude fixed to a base (Fig 13). Alternative reconstructions in which lion heads are slotted vertically or obliquely into the ground, without a base, are adduced for the Susa lions (Spycket 1988, 154, Fig 2, Pls II–III), but they differ in many respects from ours and the Tell Harmel arrangement is to be preferred. The Burrell lion is presumably one of a series that belonged to a temple. By virtue of its size it would have been

14 Set of heads from guardian lion figures: (a) 42; (b) Louvre AO 19808; (c) Louvre AO 19807.

whiskers by curvilinear incisions on raised surfaces, oval mouths lack tongues and, with the exception of the incisors, teeth are ground flat. Similarities extend to such minor details as the runnels which border furrowed noses and ribbed lappets that depend from the ears onto the cheeks. Subsidiary differences include the absence of dot rosettes on the Louvre heads; the iris of Fig 14c occupies the whole of the eye unlike the centrally placed bosses of the Burrell lion eyes and it has but one mane plate. These variations are perhaps to be expected on objects which were not made in moulds and may not have formed pairs originally. It follows that dimensions will not be exactly the same for all aspects of these lions, but measurements of intact elements (Table 2) serve to show that they could have comprised a coherent set.

Since there is no information on how the Burrell lion head arrived in the collection, it is currently only on the basis of this stylistic analysis that it may be attributed to the Hôtel Drouot lot. There are clearly many more features that unite the Burrell head with those in the Louvre than with any other lion for which detailed information is available.

Parrot quite rightly contrasted the naturalism of the Tell Harmel lions with the stylized treatment of the Louvre examples. He attributed this to 'Hurrian coarseness' and postulated that they came from the same or a similar source on the middle or upper Tigris River. The later examples from the courtyard of the Ishtar Temple at Nuzi which he adduces in support of his case however are quite grotesque by comparison (Starr 1939, Pl 109). They are reminiscent of the terracotta lions set up as a group of four or six in a temple at Susa (Amiet 1966,

292–5, Figs 218–9). The Burrell and Louvre heads in fact have much more in common with the Tell Harmel lions and it would seem that more schematized types with exaggerated features were made beyond South Mesopotamia proper.

What we may now comprehend as relatively minor differences between the Burrell-Louvre group and the Tell Harmel lions on the other hand may be of chronological significance. Thus, it has been argued that more schematized renderings of figures belong to the less unified times of King Samsu-iluna (1749–1712 BC) of Babylon and that naturalistic ones were in fashion in highly centralized earlier times (Muscarella 1981a, 115). Apart from inferences from political conditions, the argument is based on general considerations of stylistic homogeneity in the reign of Hammurabi (1792–1750 BC) and more specifically on a few stratified relief plaques from Nippur. A naturalistic lion's head from the palace at Mari lends support to such a scheme, though it could also be much earlier (Parrot 1959, Pl XXVII). If we consider this development normative for coroplasts fashioning large-scale terracottas throughout South Mesopotamia, an assumption yet to be proved, then the Burrell head may come from a guardian lion figure of about the time of Samsu-iluna. The Louvre lions however have been dated to the Larsa period in the first two centuries of the second millennium BC (Strommenger & Hirmer 1964, Pl 167) and Spycket would allow a late 3rd millennium BC date for the Susa examples (1988, 156). The paucity of secure and independent chronological evidence cautions against stylistic inferences from general political conditions and an overly narrow dating for the lions.

Table 2. Selected measurements (cms) of the Burrell and Louvre lion heads.

	42 Fig 14a	AO19808 Fig 14b	AO19807 Fig 14c
Preserved Ht	53.5	59.0	51.0
Hair line to nose tip	17.0	16.0	23.5
Ear-hole diam	1.5	0.08/9	1.15
W. of mouth	20.0	25.0	20.5
W. of (upper) mane base	32.0	34.0	25.0

43 Supplicant Figure 28.54

Middle Elamite? (Late) second millennium BC. Unprovenanced.

Standing figure with hands, now missing, once raised or clasped under chin. Beardless, disproportionately large head with narrow, oval eyes set high on forehead beneath flat headdress with notched border, broken frontal peak and perhaps a tassel at the back. Legs and one knee are articulated. The figure stands against a waist-high plinth with worn base. Cast *bronze*, corroded.

Height 0.086 m Width 0.025 m

Hannah 1953, 112–3, Fig 1.

Acquired Winifred Williams, 1951.

The posture of this figure becomes common during the Ur III–Old Babylonian periods in South Mesopotamia, Elam and later in Syria when it is used by human supplicants and divine intermediaries in the presentation of a person to a deity (Frankfort 1939a, Pls XXV–XXIX, XLI–XLII; Strommenger & Hirmer 1964, Pl XXIX. 165). The intermediaries have raised, not clasped hands, and, since they too are deities, horns of divinity. Breakage prevents certainty but the slight peak at the centre of the roll over the forehead does not appear to represent horns of divinity, nor does it occur in the otherwise similar hair plaits wound over the top of heads (Börker-Klähn 1972, 2–9, Figs 1–5, 8–13, 19). This distinctive knot is also lacking to the otherwise similar rolled rim on the head of a copper or bronze anthropomorphic cosmetic container which by its associated(?) needle belongs to the Early Dynastic period in Sumer (Muscarella 1981a, 196–7, Fig 160). Its attitude nonetheless is akin to Sumerian or Babylonian intermediaries.

Intermediaries however, like those from Ur (Braun-Holzinger 1984, Pl 35), are normally fully clothed and this discrepancy is but one of several that render an identification of the figure far from certain. Its over-large head, narrow eyes, flat cap with rolled edge and supporting plinth are all unusual features within Sumerian metal sculpture traditions. An Early Dynastic III period imported figurine at Mari demonstrates that the posture and ritual nudity were known outside South Mesopotamia earlier (Parrot 1968, Pls B.1, IV–VI), but the style is quite different and as the Syrian figures from Judeidah show, the outstretched hands held spears or the like (Frankfort 1970, 242, Fig 278). Females were frequently depicted nude in metal statuary, males less so. The absence of breasts and hair below the cap suggest that this is a male; the area around the hips is too damaged to be helpful in revealing its intended sex. Although some Sumerian figures stand on a flat base, most have tenons for slotting into bases, staffs of other materials and the like. There is no structural need for the atypical plinth at the back so presumably it forms an integral part of the composition. Sumerian metal statuary is normally free-standing, but there is a panel behind a seated figure from Susa which extends above the body to support snakes slithering over its top (Amiet 1966, Fig 233). This remarkable Susa figure calls attention to the rich tradition of metal production in neighbouring Elam, a region which transformed many Sumerian postures into a local idiom.

The temple of Inšušinak at Susa has yielded a

series of metal figurines that more closely resemble the Burrell sculpture. The series belongs to the second half of the second millennium BC and it includes one with raised arms and a cap(?) with projecting tuft over the forehead (Amiet 1966, Pl 326). Posture and headdress details are similar to our figure therefore. Amiet suggests that its lower flat body was meant to be inserted into something else and this is suggestive for the plinth on our figure, though the clearly articulated front of the body means that it was not entirely encased like, presumably, the Susa example. Others from the same temple are partly nude and wear flat caps with rolled borders (Braun-Holzinger 1984, Pls 48.233, 240). Since caps with such peaks are a feature of headdresses in second millennium Elam, perhaps consisting of material wound round hair combed forward (cf Amiet 1966, Fig 339; Börker-Klähn 1975, 9, Fig 19) our figure may represent an Elamite priest or votary of that period.

44 Administrative Tablet 28.81

Middle Assyrian; Tukulti-Ninurta I (1243–1207 BC). Unprovenanced.
Tablet of light-coloured unbaked *clay*, inscribed in cuneiform Akkadian.
Length 0.06 m Width 0.05 m Thickness 0.018 m
Unpublished.

Transliteration

1. 1 UD [ZA]BAR
   ša 3 × [   ]
      6 MA.NA [   ]
   ša [   ] × × [   ] ×
5. ša × [   ]
   a-na [   ] É [   ]-ni
   ma-a [   ]
      še × [   ] ×
   ša É.GAL-lim [   ] ×
10.   ša š[u?   ] × en nu?
   pu-[   ] × su?
   i-na-šu
   ˹PAP-˺ᵈUTU
   ÌR LUGAL
15. ša UGU É.GAL-lim
   ša qa-ab-li šap-˹li–tu˺
   a-na É LUGAL ša-ka-ni
   ta-ad-na-áš-šu
   ú-tar-ra ṭup-pu-šu
20. i-hap-pe
   ITI ku-zal-lu U₄.10.KAM
   li-mu ˹U-EN-gab-be
   DUMU LUGAL
   ˹DINGIR-SIG₅ É AGRIG
25. i-pu-ul
   a-na le-e pa-ni-e × × ×

Translation

One [   ] of bronze, of 3 [   ], 6 minas [   ] of/which [   ] of/which [   ] to [   ] house [   ] saying: ['   ] of the palace [   ] of/which [   ] they bear liability(?) for it'. Uṣur-Shamash servant of the king who (is) in charge of the palace gave to him the lower belt(?) to place in the king's house. When he brings (it) back, he may break his tablet. Month Kuzallu, 10th day, eponym year of Adad-bel-gabbe, son of the king. Ili-damiq paid back the steward's house. It was recorded(?) on a previous (waxed) writing board.

In the Late Bronze Age, when the Assyrians had overthrown foreign overlords, they built up a powerful kingdom centred on two main cities, Ashur and Kar-Tukulti-Ninurta, beside the river Tigris in northern Iraq. Tukulti-Ninurta I (1243–1207 B C), to whose reign this clay tablet is dated, was one of their most famous kings, for whom a personal epic was composed in praise of his valiant achievements in war and peace. He conquered Babylon, captured its Kassite king, ruled Babylonia for seven years, and campaigned extensively abroad. New palaces and temples of great splendour were built with the riches he won.

Many clay records have been excavated from both those cities to reveal the activities of his royal administration. As this record mentions, however, clay was not the only medium: waxed writing boards, which never survive in soil, were also common. The cuneiform text is written with a combination of signs standing for a syllable, and logographic signs; the latter stand for a whole word and are given here in capital letters. The language is semitic Akkadian, in the dialect known as Middle Assyrian. This administrative record concerns responsibility for an item of bronze, and probably comes from one of the king's palaces.

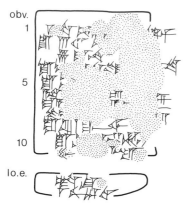
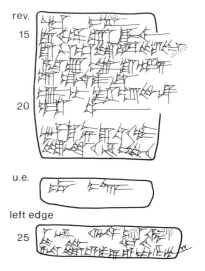

15   Middle Assyrian tablet (S. Dalley).

It was Ashurnasirpal II (883–859 BC) who, with the assistance of craftsmen and labourers captured in his many campaigns, established a subtly new type of palace at the foot of the *ziggurat* on the acropolis of Nimrud, Biblical Calah. His father had employed glazed clay slabs for architectural decoration but these were on a small scale. Inspired by earlier Assyrian reliefs on stone obelisks, that is tapered square pillars, and Neo-Hittite palace decoration, Ashurnasirpal II turned to a form of gypsum known as Mosul marble which he had carved with low relief scenes and placed in continuous friezes along the lower walls of his palace. It was a practice that was emulated by virtually all his successors. His *leitmotif* was a sacramental one involving repeated rituals in front of the sacred tree in order to demonstrate that the king partook of divine power to ensure the fertility of his domains. Our attendant's head (45) comes from such a ritual composition. Only a small number of slabs in the Throne Room are devoted to other themes such as war and hunting, and these were subsequently to dominate Assyrian palace murals.

Foreign rulers came to Ashurnasirpal's and other Assyrian palaces to offer tribute, to witness pacts, as hostages or as prisoners in fetters. There they were confronted with endless murals that made explicit to illiterates the might of the god Ashur and his earthly representative, the Assyrian king, and the futility of resistance. One of the purposes of these reliefs therefore was propaganda, and this goal helps to explain the growth of warfare as the proper subject matter for the murals. The beseiged city was a favoured motif and in this, as in all the other battle scenes, the conclusion is never left in doubt.

Except for the immense, monstrous guardian figures that stood at the entrances to palaces, the quasi-mythical content of Ashurnasirpal's timeless decorations increasingly gave way to a factual account of the deeds of the kings. This secularisation with captions and scenery supplied to lock events in time, ceaselessly depict military campaigns with their marching camps (48), the mighty Assyrian army (51,53), beseiged cities in the act of capitulating, victories rather than battles, taking of prisoners and booty (47) as well as, though less frequently, hunting exploits and building enterprises. They give no hint that the palace was also the burial place of members of the royal family who were laid to rest, with spectacular gold jewellery, beneath its floors.

Most extant sculptures come from two palaces in the fabled Nineveh, some 25 km upstream from Nimrud and opposite modern Mosul. This was one of the largest cities of the Ancient Near East and Assyria's capital for most of the 7th century BC. It was made splendid by Sennacherib's imported labour with, for example, an aqueduct, a 'bridge of burnt brick and white limestone', parks, widened squares and streets, 'portals patterned after a Hittite palace', monumental bronze images – now cast locally — and stone reliefs dragged in by the conquered.

The palaces of Sennacherib and Ashurbanipal on the Kouyunjik acropolis north of the Khosr River which flows through the city were partly excavated in the 19th century. They comprised novel, open arrangements of rooms and long inclined passages ideally suited for the display of sumptuous reliefs. As veritable treasure houses of pictorial information, they complement the extensive Royal Library found there by Layard. This was gathered by Ashurbanipal (668–627 BC) to whom our feathered archers and Elamite (**49,50,52**) should be assigned. They belong therefore to the last flourishing period of Assyrian art, but they are so fragmentary that they cannot do justice to the scope, sensitivity and, in the famous Lion Hunt scenes, thematic breakthroughs achieved under the tutelage of this learned ruler. Many of the reliefs were damaged by the Medes and other highlanders from the east in the sack of Nineveh in 612 BC, after which Assyria vanished into the realms of obscurity and misunderstanding.

45 Royal Attendant's Head 28.35

Neo-Assyrian; Ashurnasirpal II, 883–859 BC. From Room C, the North-West Palace, Nimrud.

Head of a male with long hair curled at his shoulders and wearing an *ankh*-shaped earring. Faces left; top border of robe incised with hatched decoration. Cut from a large slab of *gypsum*.

Height 0.47 m Width 0.46 m

Weidner 1951, 138; Exh. Glasgow 1949, No 27a; 1951 No 27; Reade 1965, 131; Meuszynski 1976a, 441, 1976b, 42–3, 1981, 29, Pl 4; *McLellan Galleries*, 9, left; Marks 1983, 29, Fig 4.

Acquired (ex. Coll Seymour, Wilts) Spink & Son, 1947.

The highly stylized, flat rendering of this head is characteristic of the reign of Ashurnasirpal II. He is the first Assyrian king known to have lined the walls of a royal palace with stone murals. Beardless males of this kind are usually shown as the king's personal attendants, standing beside him, offering him drink, fly whisk in hand (Strommenger & Hirmer 1964, Pl 194).

Meuszynski (1981, 29), following Reade (1965, 131), has identified the head as cut from relief slab 8 in Room C, a small chamber of the king's North-West palace at Nimrud. Guarded by colossal winged human-headed lions placed in its entrance, this small chamber was located at the end of the immensely long Throne Room, some 55 m from the throne. While the Throne Room itself contained a mixture of warlike and religious scenes, Room C was repetitively panelled with winged genies fertilising sacred trees. Our head may belong to an exceptional, poorly preserved scene amongst these. It comprises three orthostats in which the king, holding a bowl aloft and resting his other hand on his bow, is flanked by a pair of courtiers and winged genies (Fig 16). In this reconstruction, the Burrell head belongs to the attendant with a fly whisk who stands before the king, a scene that is repeated in Room G of the palace (Meuszynski 1981, Pl 8). As just stated, the composition is exceptional in Room C and it was probably meant to balance the one behind the throne at the other end of the hall where the king is also centrally placed.

There are two somewhat unusual subsidiary features of this attendant's head, its earring and the absence of a necklace. Beardless attendants normally have long drop-shaped earrings. This smaller type of earring is worn by winged genies in the Throne Room, by tribute bearers and occasionally by the king (*ibid* Pls 1, 2, 5, 6). It appears on attendants in smaller scale scenes in which Ashurnasirpal receives prisoners (Layard 1853, Pls 23–4) or at the conclusion of a bull hunt (Paley 1976, Pl 18b) for example. In contrast to this head, all similar figures wear a single or double-stranded necklace. These differences are probably due to the fact that inferior workmen exercised a certain degree of flexibility, or carelessness, in the execution of endlessly repeated minor details. More significant perhaps is the

16 Reconstructed position of **45** in Room C of Ashurnasirpal's North-West palace at Nimrud (*from* Meuszynski 1981, Pl 4).

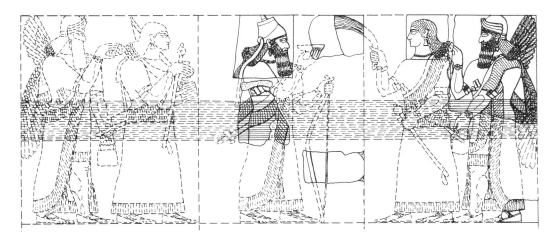

fact that Meuszynski has apparently linked the adjacent genie with this head by traces of the former's hand or pine cone behind the attendant's haircurls. There are now no traces of such connecting features on the slab and so its original position within the palace is still not entirely certain.

46 Inscribed Slab Fragment 28.78

Neo-Assyrian; Ashurnasirpal II, 883–859 BC. From the North-West Palace, Nimrud.

Two lines of a cuneiform inscription have been cut from a monumental slab of *gypsum*. Translation: '. . . the exalted prince, worshipper (of the great gods) . . . clothed with splendour . . .' (C.J. Gadd).
Height 0.043 m Length 0.19 m Thickness 0.009 m
Sotheby's 16 I 1956, 13.91; Wells 1958a, 438.4.
Acquired F. Partridge & Son, 1956.

The phraseology of these extracts is typical of the colourful and inspired royal titulary of Ashurnasirpal II. This is evident from a fuller extract:
'I am Ashurnasirpal, the obedient prince, the worshipper of the Great Gods, the fierce dragon, the conqueror of all cities and mountains to their full extent, the king of rulers who tames the dangerous enemies, the (one) crowned with glory, the (one) unafraid in battle, the relentless lion, who has shaken resistance, the king (deserving) of praise, the shepherd, protector of the world, the king whose command blots out mountains and seas, who forced into compliance fierce kings from the East and West, at his very approach' (Paley 1976, 130).

Such texts were compiled from a number of sources under the direction of either a renowned scribe or priest (*ibid* 118). They form a preamble to annalistic narratives of Ashurnasirpal's

campaigns inscribed over, beside and between the registers that comprise the seemingly endless rows of murals that depicted sacred rituals, battles and conquests in his palace at Nimrud. As few were literate, scribes presumably read these accounts to visitors and others, though the need to record deeds in writing was so strong in Mesopotamia that this alone may have sufficed to justify the incessant repetition of these texts.

Layard is known to have cut pieces like this from larger slabs that carried little or no decoration. It is likely to have been taken from one of the recensions of Ashurnasirpal's Standard Inscription.

47 Two Scribes 28.33

Neo-Assyrian; Ashurbanipal 668–627 BC. From the North Palace or Southwest Palace Court XIX, Nineveh.

Two scribes facing right tally captured booty or enemy prisoners (not visible) in a southern landscape with palm trees. They are rendered in depth but of equal size, a beardless scribe positioned in front of one with a square-cut beard. Both hold aloft a stylus between thumb and clenched right hand, and in their left hands small, hinged dyptichs, rectangular in shape and with a central ladder-patterned divison. The lower left and right corners are broken. Cut from a large slab of *gypsum*.
Remaining Height 0.182 m Width 0.15 m Thickness 0.016 m
McLellan Galleries 10; Weidner 1951, 136, Fig 1; Vogel 1959, cover; Hrouda 1965, Pl 57.4; Marks 1983, 29, Fig 5. Exh. Glasgow 1949, No 132; *Hayward* 42–50. 334.

Scribes accompanied the Assyrian armies on campaigns and, as shown here, one of their chief roles was to make a tally of captured spoil and prisoners. They are characteristically rendered

in pairs, but this representation is unusual in that both scribes hold writing boards whereas normally one is shown writing cuneiform in the traditional manner on a board and his partner, usually beardless, the relatively new and much more convenient Aramaic alphabetic script with reed pen on a scroll. They occur on Assyrian reliefs from the reign of Tiglath-Pileser III (744–725 BC) (Strommenger & Hirmer 1964, Pl 218, above) as well as in paintings (Hrouda 1965, Pls 42–3), and scribes with tablets may be depicted even earlier on reliefs at Marash in south central Turkey (Akurgal 1949, Pl XLII). Scribes are most common on murals of the later reigns of Sennacherib and Ashurbanipal, graphic testimony to the increase of bureaucracy in 7th century Assyria (Paterson 1912, Pls 17, 37, 38, 41, 52, 54, 55, 61). Our fragment comes from a scene which originally depicted the scribes counting booty or captives on the right. The palm indicates a southern setting, either Babylonia or Elam, and the style of the hair a 7th century date. Hrouda assigns it to the reign of Ashurbanipal (1965, Pl 57.4).

Of special importance are the details concerning writing techniques. Each scribe holds his stylus in a clenched fist with pressure exerted by the thumb, not for writing, but because they are shown intently counting. Scribes on the Marash reliefs also hold similar writing implements aloft, but in those cases the gesture is a formal salutation to seated dignataries (Akurgal 1949, Pl XLIIa). Square-ended styli of copper, ivory and bone have been found at Nimrud (Mallowan 1966, 162–3, Pls 96–8). In his other hand each scribe holds an object that Weidner interpreted as a clay tablet (1951, 137). There are no examples with central ladder patterns as here and his suggestion that they are symbolic of the way the script would have been laid out is unconvincing in view of the realism that is typical of Neo-Assyrian relief sculptures. They are better explained as pocket-sized notebooks, with the 'ladder' pattern representing raised central hinges.

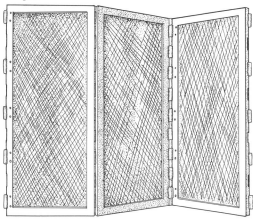

17 Reconstruction of multi-leaved drawing board showing scratched, recessed panels to secure wax and the arrangement of the hinges (*after* Howard 1955, 17, Fig 10).

Such notebooks or writing boards have been recovered from Nimrud (Mallowan 1966, 278, Pl 257) and other Assyrian sites. They consist of boards with raised margins and scored underside to secure wax that would receive the inscribed signs prior to transfer to clay tablets or other materials for permanent record (*cf* Fig 17). Large, multiple leaved boards, or polytyches, of the time of Sargon II (721–705 BC) (Mallowan 1966, 153–6) were used for the lengthy text series, *Enuma Anu Enlil* and they bore inscriptions identifying writing boards as *$^{is}le'u$* in Akkadian (Wiseman 1955, 7). According to the occurrence of this word, writing boards were known from Akkadian times and they must have been widespread for they were used by scribes in making endless lists. The earliest extant example comes, somewhat surprisingly, from the Ulu Burun (Kaş) shipwreck off the southern coast of Turkey (Bass 1987, 731) Dating to *c* 1300 BC, the wood and ivory hinged 'folding writing tablet' in Homer's words (Iliad VI, 169) provides strong evidence that the richly laden ship transported high-ranking orientals, probably from the Levant, for scribes were an elite body of men and writing boards are not known in the Aegean area. When not in use they were carried with the leaves folded together to protect the writing, as shown on a relief of Bar-Rekub of Sam'al in which the scribe stands before the king with his writing board folded under his arm. (Frankfort 1970, 305, Fig 358).

Extant fragments from Nimrud still contained traces of beeswax which rested in the central depressed area of each 'page'. References to such wax-coated writing boards (CAD, *sv* *$^{is}le'u$*) describe them as made from tamarisk, cyprus, cedar and walnut; special ones existed in ivory, like Sargon's polytych, silver, gold and lapis lazuli (Wiseman 1955, 3).

Howard's reconstruction of an ivory polytych (1955: see here Fig 17) has the hinges protruding on the interior, just as the hinges on the Ulu Burun (Kaş) diptych and as is shown realistically on a Sennacherib relief (Wiseman 1955, Pl 111.2). The sculptor of the Burrell fragment has failed to render these hinges in relief, but the central 'ladder' can hardly be anything else. Writing board details were frequently schematized and only once, in a Sennacherib sculpture, are the raised borders of each page rendered clearly (Smith 1938, Pl XLVII).

There are at least two other scenes of bearded and shaven scribes recording on tablets. One shows Ashurbanipal receiving captives and spoil from the Elamite town of Dîn-Sharri (Gadd 1936, Pl 34), one of the cities of King Um-manaldash (640–639 BC). It was found where it had fallen from the Upper Chamber of Room V in the North Palace, but unlike the Burrell fragment it lacks all background detail. The other belongs to poignant scenes from Room M in the North Palace in which Ashurbanipal accepts the surrender of his brother Shamash-shum-ukin of Babylon (667–648 BC) (Barnett 1976, Pl XXXV). In this also, the 'ladder' patterns in the centre of the writing boards are simplified versions of the hinges that project in more detailed reliefs. It has been suggested that these and other scribes writing on scrolls were in fact war artists, but the identical pairing of bearded and beardless officials on the Burrell and Dîn-Sharri reliefs, each with stylus in the same counting posture, suggests that these repeated pairs were scribes.

48   Camp Scene   28.70

Neo-Assyrian; Ashurbanipal, 668–627 BC. From Chamber S¹, North Palace, Nineveh.

Camp scene with on left, the interior of a tent, on right an upper register of two horned sheep with fodder, a lower with screen incorporating two major posts, triangular crenellations and two guy ropes (incomplete). Inside the tent a soldier with pointed helmet unfastens his corselet while a bearded attendant holds his bow and quiver. Gourds and other objects hang from a post and main beam of the tent; made-up bed on the right. A border above. Cut from a large slab of *gypsum*.

Remaining Height 0.19 m   Length 0.272 m
Hannah 1956, 185–623, Fig 2; Barnett 1976, 59, Pl LXVIb.

Acquired Spink & Son, 1953.

Tents like these were characteristically pitched for officers on the march in Assyrian military campaigns and they are shown in the palace reliefs with internal details as here. The two types of tents, a Bedouin-like structure with central post support and a straight-sided tent

with knobbed posts, are rendered in greater detail on the reliefs of Ashurbanipal.

This particular fragment was cut from the central (?) register of a large camp scene found by Loftus in 1854 at Nineveh and recorded then in a drawing by Boutcher (Gadd 1936, 134, Pl 29a) (Fig 18). If Gadd is correct in assigning a fragment in Baghdad to this relief (there are no overlaps), then the whole clearly depicts a large fortified camp erected during one of Ashurbanipal's campaigns in Elamite territory (Gadd 1948, 19–21, Pl V). Together, these fragments show some of the most detailed scenes known of Assyrian camp life in which pigs(?) are also feeding to the left of the tent and there is a horse below. The screens may well surround the Commandant's or Royal Quarters in which case the occupant of the tent must be highly ranked in the Assyrian army. The adjoining upper frieze, now in Berlin, shows further detailed scenes of camp life including butchers at work and dromedaries. The Baghdad piece, which may belong, shows Elamite prisoners eating in the registers below the fortified camp (Barnett 1976, Pl LXVIc). The crenellated wall that surrounds it (Fig 18) is clearly no temporary affair and hence this may rather be a military outpost or fort of the kind known to have existed on the borders of Elam. The fragment therefore belongs to a large composition devoted to Ashurbanipal's Elamite campaigns. It decorated Upper Chamber S¹ (Fig 19) of his palace for retirement in Nineveh (see below, **49**, **50**).

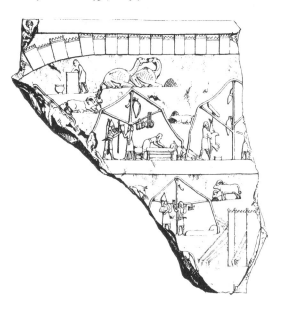

18 Boutcher's drawing shows the original position of Burrell relief **48** in the depiction of a military outpost (*from* Gadd 1936, Pl 29a).

19 Part of the conjecturally restored elevation of the North Palace at Nineveh. Reliefs **48-50** may once have adorned the walls of the room above the entrance hall (*after* Barnett 1976, Fig 12).

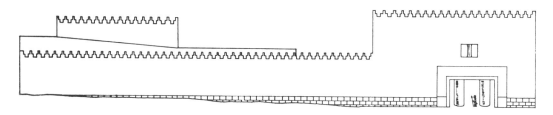

for cutting from larger *gypsum* slab; two metal-filled holes above and below.
Remaining Height 0.237 m   Width 0.094 m
Thickness 0.036 m
Hannah 1953, 350–20; Barnett 1976, 56, Pl LXII(i).
Acquired John Hunt, 1950.

**50   Archer With Feathered Head-
       dress   28.61**

Neo-Assyrian; Ashurbanipal 668–627 B C.
From Chamber S¹ North Palace, Nineveh
(?).
Archer with feathered headdress comprised of vertical feathers and tasseled headband, Assyrian-style, square-cut beard and short, curled moustache. He faces right and holds a duck-terminal bow; some form of dress is indicated by a band from his waist over his right shoulder. Another register above with traces of one foot and an object. Cut from a large *gypsum* slab.
Remaining Height 0.165 m   Width 0.105 m
Thickness 0.044 m
Hannah 1953, 350.2, Fig 1; Barnett 1976, 56, Pl LXII(m).
Acquired John Hunt, 1952.

**49   Archer With Feathered Head-
       dress   28.38**

Neo-Assyrian; Ashurbanipal, 668–627 B C.
From Chamber S¹ North Palace, Nineveh
(?).
Archer with feathered headdress, square-cut beard and moustache. He faces right and carries a duck-terminal bow. A band extends across his chest and over his right shoulder and a vertical fringe depends from a three-stranded belt. Chipped and worn; beard partially incised. Demarcation lines near edges

These two fragments were probably cut from a single remarkable series of sculptures depicting Persian auxiliary bowmen, according to Barnett (1976, 55), marching to an Assyrian triumphal reception in celebration of the defeat of the Elamites. They may originally have been located in Ashurbanipal's North Palace, but certainty is not possible becaue of defective recording methods. Reade, for example, suggests that they may have come from Room XXII of Senna-cherib's Palace because it is the only one in which Layard mentions having found feather-capped figures (1967, 43 n.7: the 'Glasgow' fragments do not join as stated). Not all such figures are archers however; feathered headdres-ses were also donned by musicians (cf Calmeyer 1970). Feathered archer slabs are now scattered in several museums including London, Paris and Venice. They are assembled by Barnett (1976, Pl LXII) and his attribution is largely followed here.

In his second report of the Assyrian Excava-tion Fund for 1855, William Kennett Loftus wrote:

'Above this entrance wall and its adjoining chambers there was formerly another story, the first upper rooms yet discovered in Assyria. This with its sculptural slabs had fallen into the rooms below . . . The slabs have been a good deal injured in their fall by coming into contact with blocks of masonry' (quoted in Barnett 1976, 18).

The rooms refered to, S and S¹, comprise the lower and upper rooms of the principal entrance in the northwest corner of the North Palace at Nineveh (Fig 19). Two massive columns were set inside this entrance after the North Syrian manner. Above the spacious porch was a large room, probably with colonnaded window as shown in Fig 19. Although nothing is known of its internal arrangements nor the position of the murals, certain scenes are acknowledged to have come from S¹ because W. Boutcher, who illu-strated so many of the sculptures while working with Loftus, annotated many of his drawings with this information. They include Ashur-banipal hunting and pouring libations over slain lions, the assault and capture of cities such as Hamanu, the surrender of the Elamites and the

famous banquet scene in the gardens where the head of the Elamite Te-umman gruesomely dangles from a tree branch (Strommenger & Hirmer 1964, Pl 241). Barnett has ascribed other slabs, including the Burrell pieces, to this room by virtue of style and composition. Gadd had previously suggested that two others in the British Museum came from Room I which con-tained reliefs of a battefield in Elam with the decapitation of Ituni, an Elamite officer (1936, 194–5).

More recently, Erika Bleibtreu has suggested that a fragment in Istanbul listed by Barnett in his study of this series from the North Palace (1976, Pl 62n) belongs to Room XXXIII of the South-West Palace at Nineveh (pers comm 2.VIII.1988). Some of the stone used to decorate the walls of this room includes white inclusions which show up as distinctive spots on the surface. Our 49 is made of pinkish gypsum with some colour depletion, but no white spots on the surface. The other member of this pair also lacks white spots and hence they probably come from another room, perhaps chamber S¹ in the North Palace.

The two Burrell fragments should belong with twelve grouped together by Barnett. The archers are all shown proceeding to the right in narrow registers, some beside a stream and others below Assyrian *kalû* (lamentation) priests with fish tail hats. On better preserved fragments in the Louvre and in Rome the archers wear skirts with fringed edges that fall between their knees, boots and quivers simply decorated with bars and crossed bands. There is no accompanying in-scription to identify these most unusual archers. Barnett's suggestion that they are Persian tribes-men who once served with the Elamites but subsequently joined the Assyrians seems fanciful but is not without merit since it does help to explain the combination of exotic feathered headdress and Assyrian-style coiffure. Others in these scenes are clearly Elamite according to the style of their hair and beards.

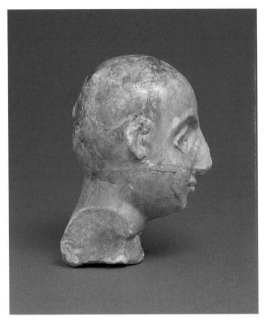

25 Head of Worshipper Statue (profile) (*see* pages 47–8)

25 Head Of Worshipper Statue (frontal) (*see* pages 47–8)

42 Lion Head (*see* pages 65–6)

47   Two Scribes (*see* pages 74–7)

57   Inscribed Brick (*see* page 85)

51   Assyrian Soldier In Palm Grove (*see* page 81)

60 Cauldron Protome
In The Shape Of A Bull's Head
(*see* pages 90–2)

96 Fenestrated Axehead (*see* pages 123–4)

62 Part Of A Standard (*see* page 95)

69 Decorated Pin Terminal (*see* page 99)

79 Wild Goat Handle (*see* page 104)

51 Assyrian Soldier In Palm Grove 28.65

Neo-Assyrian; Sennacherib or Ashurbanipal 704–627 BC. From Nineveh; probably the South-West Palace.

Head of an Assyrian soldier among palm trees. He has a square-cut beard, curled moustache and wears a long pointed helmet with ear guards. Traces of a weapon or quiver behind. A label on reverse reads:- 'A head of a warrior dug in the excavations in Nineveh in the year (tho)usand eight hun(dred) (a)nd forty nine . . . by . . . Hor[m]uzd = (?) Rassam'. Cut from a large relief slab of *gypsum*. Remaining Height 0.15 m   Width 0.10 m
Hannah 1953, 351.24; *Hayward*, 43.335.
Acquired John Hunt, 1952.

During 1849, the year in which this slab was found according to the label on the reverse, excavations were concentrated in Sennacherib's South-West Palace at Kouyunjik in Nineveh. Rassam is credited as the discoverer but it was Layard who had the *firman* (permit) for work here and Rassam did not undertake his own major excavations before 1853 in the North Palace of Ashurbanipal. Part of the confusion may have arisen because in 1852 or 1853 Rassam sent back to England sculptures from the South-West palace previously discovered by Layard. Although built by Sennacherib, this palace was occupied by Ashurbanipal who set up his own sculptures in it, sometimes re-working those of his predecessor.

The pointed helmet with bordered ear-guard, the most datable element of the fragment, was prevalent throughout the Sargonid period (Hrouda 1965, Pl 23.12). The soldier is depicted in a South Mesopotamian or Elamite setting where palm groves were common. Both Sennacherib and Ashurbanipal executed reliefs of their many southern campaigns. It could belong to either reign and probably represents an archer.

When helmeted archers are shown in action their bowstrings normally pass in front of their faces (Paterson 1912, Pl 45). The rims of their great shields also usually pass along the beard (*ibid* Pl 55), so this archer is probably not in action but rather one of the innumerable guards or attendants conducting prisoners to be counted or presented to the king after victory in battle (e.g. *ibid* Pls 57–8; Frankfort 1970, 178, Fig 203).

51

52

52   Elamite Archer   28.73

Neo-Assyrian; Ashurbanipal, 668–627 BC.
From South-West Palace, Nineveh.
Upper body and head of Elamite archer facing left.
Figure with cropped beard stands with his bow
drawn and his back to us. His quiver, full of arrows,
is decorated with horizontal zones, the uppermost
with an X-design. His short-cut hair is tied with a
headband. White speckled *gypsum* (?fossilizitrous
limestone).
Remaining Height 0.147 m   Width 0.123 m
Unpublished.
Acquired Spink & Son, 1953.

The distinctive headband, short hair and
trimmed beard identify this archer as an Elamite
and, because Elamite soldiers with these features
did not enter the Assyrian army, as a foe of
Assyria. Such archers are frequent enough in the
reliefs of Ashurbanipal, but in keeping with the
artistic policies of the reign, if not shown in acts
of submission they are usually depicted in
retreat, frightened and without pausing to
release an arrow as here. This archer therefore
belongs to a rarer scene in which the Elamites are
shown as active combatants. One setting in
which this occurs is an Assyrian assault on an
Elamite city where defenders are shown releas-
ing arrows from their battlement stations. An
example of this type of composition is the
conquest of the city of Hamanu (Strommenger &
Hirmer 1964, Pl 237); in contrast, the three

archers still fighting in the bottom register in the
Til Tubē battle have more elaborate haircurls
and quivers (Paterson 1912, Pls 62–4). These
sculptures come from the North and South-
West Palaces of Nineveh respectively, but as
Ashurbanipal redecorated the latter, the distinc-
tion is hardly conclusive. Its peculiar white-
speckled surface suggests that the slab may have
originally adorned the walls of Room XXXIII of
the South-West Palace as part of the Til Tubē
scene (E. Bleibtrau, pers. comm. 2 VIII. 1988).
That scene however is generally carved in better
quality gypsum and the hair and beards of the
Elamites are carefully modelled rather than cursorily incised as here.

**53   Mounted Soldiers Parading
Right**   28.77

Neo-Assyrian; Ashurbanipal, 668–627 BC.
Probably from Nineveh.
Upper parts of two bowmen riding to right; head of
one horse. Each wears a pointed helmet and
supports a bow and quiver on his back; the left
rider also holds a spear inclined forward. The
horse's head is decked with elaborate regalia (very
worn) and a crescent-shaped plume. Cut from a
large slab of *gypsum*, now worn.
Remaining Height 0.11 m   Length 0.26 m   Thickness 0.017 m
Sotheby's 16.I.1956, 13.91; Wells 1958a, 438.3;
Reade 1972, Pl XLa; Barnett 1976, 62, Pl LXXI(r).
Acquired F. Partridge & Son, 1956.

The pointed helmets with developed ear-guards, the hairstyles and the full, crescentic horse plumes belong to the 7th century BC, specifically to the time of Ashurbanipal. So worn is this fragment that little in the way of stylistic detail is left. Its major interest lies in the small scale of the figures. That the remnant comes from an unusually small relief does not necessarily follow however since tiny figures are included in slabs of normal size in the 7th century BC.

Commentators have suggested a number of provenances for this fragment. Least likely is the site of Nimrud, which is given in the relevant Sotheby's catalogue for 1956. Because of its small scale, Reade suggests that it may possibly have come from the throne base in Room M of the North Palace at Nineveh (1972, 111), basing this conclusion in part on the analogous small decorated sides of the throne base of Shalmaneser III (858–824 BC) at Nimrud (cf Mallowan 1966, 444–50). The principle theme there however is one of peace, and not a warlike composition as here. Barnett remained unconvinced of this ascription and he allowed that it could even come from the South-West Palace at Nineveh where reliefs of Ashurbanipal have also been found (1976, 60–2). E. Bleibtrau proposes that it could have come from Room XXII of the South-West Palace and she notes that mounted soldiers armed with bows in bowcases carried on their backs and lances only occur on reliefs of Ashurbanipal (pers comm 2.VIII.88).

54 Pazuzu Head Pendant 28.52

Assyro-Babylonian, c 750–500 BC. Unprovenanced.

Snarling lion's head with (secondary ?) perforated clay strip applied on top of head. Uneven flat back and small tenon below chin. Two horns protrude above multiple brows, the tongue is not indicated in the gaping mouth immediately below the nose and there are vertical incisions on its chin below the lower lip (beard?). Right side of face and left horn are broken. Roughly modelled, unslipped, white, *terracotta*, slightly pink on the interior.

Height 0.07 m   Width 0.036 m

Hannah 1953, 112.6; Green 1985, 76 n.13 (with incorrect Burrell number).

Acquired John Hunt, 1951.

Ancient Mesopotamians possessed a variety of amulets to ward off evil. The distinctive features of this head identify it as Pazuzu who, according to an inscribed, well preserved example supposedly from Nineveh, is 'son of Khanbu, king of the *lilû*-demons' (Ismail 1974, 125). When Pazuzu is shown complete on small plaques he is represented with horned leonine head, wings, bird's lower torso, talons, snake-like phallus and scorpion's tail. Since he was regarded as king of the evil spirits he had control over them and hence this demon was a popular apotropaic talisman. In one ritual a bronze Pazuzu was to be placed on the neck of a pregnant woman so to protect her and her unborn child from Lamashtu, a similarly rendered demon with lion head.

This menacing figure was produced in metal pendant form (Braun-Holzinger 1984, 74–9), on plaques with exorcism scenes, on stamp seals, maceheads and fibulae for use in houses, temples and in graves (Moorey 1965). Examples have been found as far away from Mesopotamia as Samos and Egypt. They occur during the Neo-Assyrian period and persisted throughout the Neo-Babylonian period into Seleucid times. This example is a badly mutilated detached-head pendant type which was most common in the 8th–7th centuries BC (cf Loud & Altman 1938, Pl 64.256 from the Temple of Nabu at Khorsabad). Thureau-Dangin (1921, 192–3) gives an incomplete list of pottery heads; BM 91875 illustrated by Campbell Thompson (1903, Pl II) with an identical perforation most resembles this.

55 Duck Weight 28.74

Mesopotamian c 2000–500 BC. Unprovenanced.

Duck with flat base and head lying on its back. Feathers of wings and head are neatly incised with herring-bone patterns. The edges of the bill are doubly incised and the circular eye sockets have lost their inlays. Brown-black *limestone*, chipping to white where struck, especially at squared end and around perimeter of base, perhaps indicating secondary use as a hammer.

Weight 1435 gr   Height 0.064 m
Length 0.153 m
Hannah 1956, 185.5.
Acquired Spink & Son, 1953.

56 Duck Weight 28.47

Assyro-Babylonian 800–600 BC (?). Unprovenanced.

Plain weight with chipped head of duck lying on its back and the bill outline incised. Round based, squared end. Chipped black *haematite*.

Weight 487.1 gr   Height 0.037 m   Length 0.07 m
Hannah 1953, 349.1.
Acquired G.F. Williams, 1952.

Modelled ducks with heads laid on their backs became popular in Mesopotamia from at least c 2250 BC, when they were used as weights. They were popular in Assyria, Babylonia and Susa, exceedingly stereotyped and sometimes bear an inscription. The latter includes certification of the actual weight (e.g. the king 'for Nanna established [its weight as] 5 minas'), dedications to deities and Sargon's royal lion.

Relatively small examples with squared ends were common at Khorsabad during the 8th–7th centuries BC (Loud & Altman 1938, Pl 61. 175–87), but the type is not confined to that time. The tips of the bills of the Khorsabad ducks extend well over half way along their backs as on **56**. Its weight accords well enough with the Babylonian standard of 1 mina (504.96 g) if one allows for the neck breakage.

The larger duck now falls rather short of 3 minas (1514 g) on the Babylonian system. Its elaborately incised facial features and wings are absent from the substantial group of weights which Unger published in 1918 (xvi–xviii, 20–29). Of the 13 recorded examples from Mallowan's excavations at Nimrud, only one was elaborately decorated. Unfortunately, this was badly damaged (Curtis 1989, 26). Greater naturalism, including the depiction of wings, is evident on later weights of the Neo-Babylonian/Achaemenid period from sites such as Sippar and Persepolis (cf Curtis 1989, 25–6, Pl XII, Fig 21). Until we have securely provenanced duck weights with incised details belonging to the more stylized Burrell type we should treat the addition of wings and other details with reserve. They may well have been added to a genuine, possibly Neo-Assyrian, weight in more recent times.

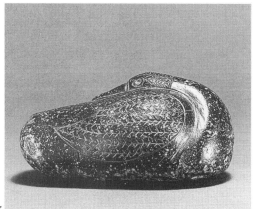

55

56

57 Inscribed Brick 28.46

Neo-Babylonian; Nebuchadnezzar II
c 604–562 BC. From the Palace of Nebuchadnezzar II, Babylon.

Moulded clay brick with seven lines of inscription
set in a slightly depressed area, 0.145 m × 0.11 m.
The inscription is translated by C.J. Gadd (or M.
Savage) as follows:

1 Nebuchadnezzar
2 King of Babylon
3 Patron of the temple E-Sagila
4 and of the temple E-Zida
5 Eldest son of Nabo-
6 polassar
7 King of Babylon

Height 0.15 m Length 0.20 m Thickness 0.072 m
Hannah 1953, 112.9.
Acquired Wm. Ohly, 1951.

Bricks of this type were incorporated into the
walls of the Southern Citadel at Babylon in large
numbers, usually repeated in a single course and
with a standardized inscription of 3, 4, 6, 7 or 8
lines. The complete inscription was made by the
impression of a pottery or metal stamp on the
soft clay of the brick which was moulded in a
wooden frame resting on reeds (Koldewey 1914,
75–87). *E-Sagila* was the large Marduk temple
which stood beside the bridge across the Euphrates River in Babylon, *E-Zida* the temple of
Nabu, patron of the scribes.

Repetitive display inscriptions like this may
have started in the second millennium BC in
Elam and Babylonia. In Assyria they were subsequently executed in stone (*cf* **46**) together with
historic and symbolic scenes, a practice not
emulated in Babylonia.

58 Female Figurine 28.21

Parthian Period; 2nd century BC–2nd
century AD. Unprovenanced.

Frontal, nude, female figurine, much worn, mended
and with head and left lower leg missing.
Disproportionately short arms with incised fingers
raised to ill-defined breasts, full hips with little suggestion of a waist and a slightly incised pubic
triangle. Folds of kneecaps are cursorily incised, but
otherwise the surface is too chipped to reveal
modelled detail. Plaque-like with minimal modelling
on reverse, feet splayed to retain figure in upright
position. Mended breaks at arms and upper left leg
give the appearance of grooves. *Bone.*

Height 0.046 m Width 0.028 m Thickness
0.008 m
Unpublished. Exh. Glasgow, 1949, No 150.
Acquired John Hunt, 1948.

Models of nude females in this posture occur
frequently in Western Asia and they are usually
thought to symbolise fertility, if not to represent
votaries or aspects of a particular goddess. They
are executed in ivory, which this resembles, at
least from the Early Dynastic III period, a date
indicated by the association of an inscription of
Mesannipadda with one from Mari (Parrot 1968,
Pls VII, VIII; *cf* also Curtis 1982, Pl 4c from
Tell Brak). They continue to be produced in
gradually increasing numbers thereafter (e.g.
Andrae 1922, 56–7, Pl 29a–e). In virtually all
instances however the craftsmanship is far finer
than is evident on this example; material and
style of these ivory figurines also remain at odds
with it.

Female figurines executed in bone and carved
with broad hips that curve out immediately
below the chest and schematized triangular feet
splayed out to provide stability are hallmarks of
a later style belonging to the Parthian period.
According to Colledge, these were mass
produced for religious purposes (1967, 225, Pl
17). Yet in the early excavations at Seleucia, only
three of the many recovered bone figurines were
found in the temple area, while others were
found in graves, predominantly belonging to
children. This led Van Ingen to support the
theory that they were dolls (1939, 44). Some
were also found in what may have been a shop.
Complete figurines normally have head wreaths

or elaborate coiffures. At Seleucia the bone figurines were not found before Parthian levels and they probably continued to be used and perhaps manufactured into Sassanian times.

Many stamped sherds were recovered from probable Sassanian levels at Nineveh (Campbell Thompson 1933, Pl LXXVII). The stamps were normally made from circular dies with a single stylized animal motif: stag, goat with tree, horse, bull and eagle are particularly popular within the figurative repertoire. It would seem that stamps like this are distinctive of northern Mesopotamia (*cf AfO* 34, 1987, 176, Figs 93–4). Adams notes that they are found only infrequently in his southern Mesopotamian survey, south of the Diyala region (1981, 234). Rectilinear stamps are uncommon and they may be a product of specific centres.

Traces of a second stamp on this fragment suggest that there were one or more rows of repeated impressions of the same stamp around the body of the jar. Two continuous friezes made from a rectangular stamp with a browsing deer are impressed in this manner around the lower part of an unprovenanced large handled jar, probably from Iran (Pope 1938, IV, Pl 186A).

Stamps regularly occur on sherds from large vessels and so they may have identified bulk products from redistributive centres and the administrative control of such products.

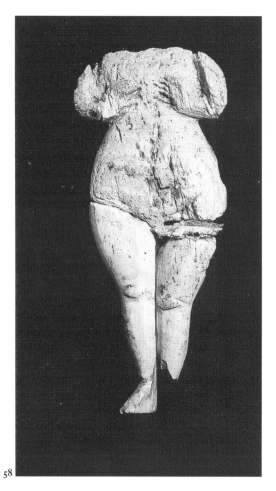

58

59 Stamped Sherd 28.82

Late Sassanian-Umayyad *c*AD 400–650.
Unprovenanced.

Body sherd from large closed pot with one complete and one partly preserved rectangular stamped impression (4 × 2.7 cm) on the exterior surface. They are from the same stamp which bears a single zebu walking left with long legs bent acutely at their joints, triangular head and hump, and large horns shown *en face*. Hard-fired pink-buff *pottery* with fine mineral inclusions.

Height 0.07 m Width 0.082 m Thickness 0.009 m
Unpublished

11 HIGHLAND METALWORK

The Assyrians have vividly described the mountainous areas and their inhabitants which lay in an arc to the east and north of Mesopotamia, in modern western Iran and southeastern Turkey. These were, 'high mountains, covered with all kinds of trees', 'whose passes were frightful, over whose areas shadows stretch as in a cedar forest' with people who 'were without equal . . . in their knowledge of riding horses' who had crops, granaries, great walled and moated cities, canals and pleasant gardens and who were ruled by 'chieftains . . . with prancing horses, swift mules, (Bactrian) camels, cattle and sheep'.

These were diverse groups of people which are here considered together because of common highland traits, greater or lesser contacts with the anciently urbanised Mesopotamian and Elamite civilisations and expertise in display metal-work which is only partially represented in the collection.

Readily available copper and other metals in eastern Turkey and the Zagros mountains of western Iran were avidly sought after by Mesopotamians and it is in these areas at Çayönü and other sites that the earliest known metal-work has been found. Enmerkar, a Sumerian *en* of the mid-3rd millennium BC, already seems to have sent a delegation into the mountains to procure precious metals from natives ostensibly for the embellishment of a temple. Even before that time, colonies of southern merchants were established at sites like Godin Tepe and trade routes carried precious lapis lazuli from distant Afghanistan and beyond.

The high valleys of the Zagros mountains are arranged like parallel funnels orientated towards the Caucasus and this topography encouraged the formation of small, easily disrupted polities and fragile exchange systems. Except where cohesive states existed, as in Urartu in eastern Turkey, or on a lesser scale in upland plains around Lake Rezaiyah and Kermanshah, the social norm in antiquity was the tribal group, often practicing transhumance and dwelling in small settlements. These were ruled over by tribal sheikhs who eventually possessed fortified manors. They were frail buffers to incomers who moved into these areas in the 2nd – early 1st millennia BC and hence this period is one of considerable cultural flux; it is exceedingly difficult to ascribe the manufacture and use of particular objects to specific his-torically-documented people.

This difficulty has been exacerbated by a veritable flood of bronze objects that appeared in the west at least from 1928, all allegedly from Luristan, a region of the Zagros mountains where clandestine and some legalized but unscientific 'excavations' were endemic. Recent studies and long overdue, properly conducted excavations, have demonstrated that such 'Luristan bronzes' are not all from this area, nor all of one period; they do show the prolific and precocious nature of bronzeworking centres in western Iran over a long period of time. We know little beyond the cemeteries of the producers of the earliest distinctive items in this tradition – weapons (80). Some bear incised names of Akkadian rulers (*c* 2300 BC) and so suggest an approximate date for many classes of objects as well as important links with Mesopotamia. Many of these could be products of the Lullu tribe which seemingly adopted some Akkadian and Summerian customs.

The zenith of this Highland metal production came in the earlier half of the 1st millennium BC. It is useful to assess it in the light of the movement of Iranian tribes and Asiatic steppe peoples into this zone. Medes, Persians, Cimmerians and Scythians are involved here and the impact on each other as well as their interaction with the high civilisations of Assyria, Urartu and Elam resulted in vigorous new animal styles, the effects of which were felt from China to Western Europe. This was accompanied, if not preceded, by the first common use of iron in these regions.

Only some 30 pieces are known from properly excavated contexts of this creative period but the major classes of production are tolerably well understood. With the elaborately decorated horse bits and harness attachments (72–76) we come close to the mobility and love of display that especially characterised Cimmerian and Scythian societies. The former supplied cavalry for the Assyrian army: the lands around Lake Rezaiyah where other tribes, if not Cimmerian themselves, lived, were famed for horses. Their warrior bands invaded well established metal-using communities with a richly developed iconographical repertoire in which animal art was dominant. The most outstanding works incorporate motifs from Phoenicia, Assyria, Iran and the Asiatic steppes, a medley which aptly reflects the mixture of highly mobile warrior peoples. More commonly, old Western Asiatic motifs like griffins were reinterpreted with a fresh vigour and severe stylisation.

The age old Mesopotamian theme of the hero between two beasts became a favourite subject of Luristan metalworkers. It dominates the 'standards' (61–64) and pinheads (68–69) where the corporeality of the Mesopotamian forms has disintegrated, to be replaced by ruthlessly fragmented images, in which natural shapes are subjected to the dictates of symmetrical compositions. These are essentially applied works of art, exuberant displays which often seem to have a greater affinity with such recurrent themes as biting animals in pre- and early Norse metalwork than with traditional Near Eastern iconography.

With unquenchable, if sometimes naive, spontaneity, most available surfaces of these and *repoussé* plaques, discs and situlae, or buckets, were transformed and embellished with fantastic creatures, often in complex associations. Found in mortuary contexts and a temple, they depict a religion that has been interpreted in many ways, frequently as a pre-Zoroastrian pantheon in which Mitra and Varuna figure, but such interpretations are speculative.

The Kingdom of Urartu (c 900–585 BC), with its centralised government, presents a contrast to this shifting world of petty tribes, some still semi-nomads, others sedentary and even urbanised, though both possessed rich metalworking traditions. A letter of the Assyrian king Sargon to the god Ashur in 714 BC gives some idea of the immense wealth in metals at the shrine of the national god of Urartu, Khaldi – large quantities of gold, silver, white bronze, iron, bronze and lead, silver chariots, native and foreign objects inlaid with same, a 'silver javelin, encrusted with gold', statues and some 100,000 kilos of scrap bronze. Surviving objects from Urartu emphasize the sacred, the royal and the heavily Assyrianising nature of this art. Fragments of thrones, shields, helmets and belts, statues and ceremonial cauldrons are the principal works, all heavily ornamented with stereotyped designs. This secondary centre affected a wide area, from Russia to Italy.

As we learn from Strabo's (d. AD 25) geography and the many columned manors of the northern Zagros, the Achaemenid Persians in turn borrowed much from the Medes. They represent the culmination of the Iranian wanderings mentioned above by winning the Median (550 BC) and the Neo-Babylonian (539 BC)

Empires. They were thus transformed from interlopers on the periphery to rulers at the centre of an expanded ancient world.

The image of a decrepit authority gleaned from biased accounts of Alexander the Great who overthrew this empire (330 BC) is rapidly moderating as we obtain more objective insights into the organisation, application of justice and cultural achievements of the Achaemenids. Theirs was an immense territory in which they successfully promoted the notion of a world unity, a concept that seems to have been alien to their Mesopotamian predecessors but one that was essential to stability and security. Quick to select ideas from subject nations and amalgamate them into a new and richer whole, as in the architectural complex of Persepolis, the Achaemenids mark a definite end of the Mesopotamian dominated era of the history of Western Asia and the beginning of its role in a much more broadly based history.

Metalwork from these highland zones in the Burrell provides selective insights into some two millennia of varied production. The high proportion attributed to the 10th–7th centuries BC reflects increased output then, no doubt due to the desire for ostentatious display that often distinguishes horse-riding warrior societies. Among the 35 objects listed below, **60**, the Urartian bull's head protome, is to be singled out for its refinement and because it possibly comes from an important, historically documented site, Van, the capital of the kingdom of Urartu. Significant because of their rarity, are a silver libation goblet (**87**) and bronze amphora with zoomorphic handle and spout (**91**).

60 Cauldron Protome In The Shape Of A Bull's Head   33.212

Urartian mid-late 8th century BC. Very probably from Toprak Kale (Lake Van), Turkey.

Socketed, horned bull's head with traced and relief details. The face has a long flat forehead, sensitively modelled with widely spaced nostrils and a long groove underneath for a small-chinned mouth. Large ears project and horns with stroked rings around their bases extend up and back. The hair consists of a raised rectangular forelock engraved with six, parallel strands, interrupted by four horizontal bands of curls. Similar curls form a ruff that extends from the ears to the neck. The eyes are in relief with two engraved outlines ending in pronounced tear ducts at either side of the eye. Pairs of traced lines on the muzzle connect the tips of the forelock with engraved wrinkles across the bridge of the nose; midway on these lines are projecting single crescents. Cast in *bronze*. The socket is now plugged with wood and X-rays show that the right horn above the break is restored with some organic substance secured to the base of the horn by a metal armature. Also possible ancient patching (see Appendix A).

Height 0.143 m   Width 0.112 m   Depth 0.113 m
Amandry 1956, 239–242, Pls XXIVd, XXVd, XXVId; Wells 1958b; 1960, 189.2, Fig 1; *Hayward*, 43; Marks 1983, 29, Fig 6.
Acquired Spink & Son, 1957.

This head matches precisely one of a group of four studied by P. Amandry (1956). Breakages, stylistic peculiarities and measurements as listed in detail by Amandry (1956, 240) are the same as his head D. In the absence of further information from Burrell sources, Amandry's reconstruction of the history of this head is the most thorough available.

Having persuasively argued that all four heads come from the same cauldron, Amandry showed that they were most likely found in 1880 at Toprak Kale in Turkey by Hormuzd Rassam who was excavating there on behalf of the British Museum. Rassam noted the discovery of 'some bronze bull's heads', two of which went to the British Museum. Two others, nearly identical, had more checkered post-excavation careers. They appeared briefly in a Spanish general history of art in 1931, and this one seems to have come to Glasgow via dealers and collectors in

New York and Paris. The fourth head is in the Walter's Art Gallery, Baltimore.

All four have distinctive rings around the bases of their horns and eyebrows with chased herring-bone patterns overhanging the eyes. One of this group retains its seating plate, shaped like a bird's wings and tail, by which it was originally fixed to a cauldron. This is missing on the Burrell head. A complete cauldron from Altin Tepe far to the west of Toprak Kale on the opposite side of Lake Van, but still within the Kingdom of Urartu, shows how these heads were fixed as four protomes beneath the rim of an immense cauldron which stood on a tall bronze tripod (Fig 20). Zoomorphic cauldron protomes of different, though related types, were produced in a number of Near East and Mediterranean centres (Muscarella 1988b, 263 n.1). Some 15 examples of the canonical Urartian type are known, none from excavations outwith Urartu.

It is generally acknowledged that the Toprak Kale group of protomes to which we may ascribe this head is the earliest of a widespread and varied series belonging to cauldrons that are known from Iran and Russia in the east to Etruria in Italy in the west (see **105**). Its 8th century BC date rests on several assumptions. Two of the most important are that stylistic development proceeded as Hanfmann suggested, from the simplification of elaborate Assyrian

patterns to an increase of plastic, cast details (1956, 212) and that the complete example from Altin Tepe comes from a tomb to be dated to the reign of Argishti II (Azarpay 1968, 52). Since the collars of the Altin Tepe protomes are more schematized than ours and more features are cast in plastic form, the Toprak Kale ones should be earlier, perhaps belonging to the time of that great builder at Toprak Kale, Rusa I (c 735–713 BC).

The Altin Tepe cauldron however does not come from controlled excavations and so its date must be treated with caution. Its intact state does imply that it came from a tomb and so we know that such enormous mixing bowls were deposited as funerary gifts, in all probability for royalty and perhaps the aristocracy. Similar cauldrons have been found in presumed royal and barbarically rich burials on other fringes of the contemporary Assyrian Empire, in Phrygia and Cyprus, and hence they were recognized expressions of political power. The most likely way in which they became fashionable was through contacts made at royal courts where, we may assume, they often formed the centrepiece of sumptuous feasts. A cauldron with sphinx and griffen protomes from a richly equipped 'royal' tomb at Salamis, Cyprus, was full of items suitable for elite gatherings, namely pottery flasks encrusted with tin (Karageorghis 1969, Pls 40, 41). The high status of these cauldrons in diverse kingdoms is also demonstrated by the association of a small example in Tumulus D at Bayinder/Elmali with a plain silver cauldron, inscribed silver ladle and silver and ivory statu-ettes (Özgen & Özgen 1988, 35.33). Similar massive cauldrons supported on tripods were used in temples, but in one revealing instance, on

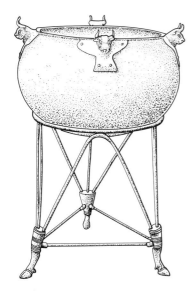

20 Cauldron and stand from Altin Tepe, Turkey (*after* Piotrovsky 1967, 40, Fig 26.1).

21 Handled bucket from Neo-Assyrian relief sculpture (*after* Hrouda 1965, Pl 19.6)

a Sargon II (*c* 722–705 BC) relief of an Urartian temple, the cauldron is deeper and it lacks protomes.

The combination of bull's head with bird's wings and tail (its original seating plate, now missing) is an odd one, but that very oddness is instructive. In Assyria, metal buckets were often embellished with such wings (Fig 21) and in other scenes the bird is replaced by the god Ashur in a winged sun disc (e.g. Strommenger & Hirmer 1964, Pl 190 second row right). Such wings had long been a suitable vehicle for divinity in the Ancient Near East and so in Urartu, where the bull was so closely identified with the national god Khaldi, the conjunction becomes understandable. Khaldi himself is often framed by a winged disc (e.g. Seidl 1988, Pls 100, 101, 103). The inspiration for the iconography of these protomes may therefore have been derived from Assyria and this process of borrowing may be regarded as one more instance of an Assyrianizing tendency which pervaded the royal arts of Urartu. Other protomes which served as handle mounts were fashioned in the shape of sirens, or birds with female bodies. Piotrovski proposed that they represent the Urartian sun god's consort, Tushpuea (1967, 37). North Syria is another possible centre to be considered in seeking the origin for the concept of zoomorphic handles mounts, for it is in this area of thriving kingdoms that winged bird attachments were used on vessels already in the late second millennium BC (Beyer 1982, 120, Fig 2).

Standards   61–64

In many ways, so-called 'standards' epitomize bronzes from Luristan. They are characterized by a high degree of stylization which was created within imaginative, yet conservative iconographical traditions. They are amongst the most numerous and, because elaborate, highly sought after bronzes to attract collectors, particularly in the west. Almost all were ultimately obtained from improperly controlled 'excavations'. Although we have complete examples, their function is still unknown. The elaborate Master-of-Animals imagery has a mythological significance that still escapes us. Thanks to limited scientific excavations in the Pusht-i Kuh region however, we have some idea of their date and how, occasionally, they were used (Muscarella 1988b, 136–41, 147–50).

Usually only the upper part survives, but there are enough extant lower sections to show how, when complete, standards formed tall, slender stands (**61**). Some were probably once connected by an internal perishable rod, but many are likely to be modern pastiches (*cf* Moorey 1971, Pl 134.177). As in these four examples, the major theme is that of a central figure with male or female characteristics grasping snarling fantastic beasts. Subsidiary motifs, especially animal heads, are often appended. Details may be abbreviated, as in the case of the circular boss inside a V on **64**. On other examples a face occurs in this position (*ibid* Pl 34.178). The simplest, **63**, lacks the normal arms of the 'master'. It belongs to a distinctive variant with a significant recurrence at the temple to Hera on the distant Aegean island of Samos, one of the very few sites outside Luristan to have produced these bronzes (Jantzen 1972, Pl 74. B 896). In spite of the fact that the concept of the central motif has a lengthy Mesopotamian and Elamite history it has been so radically altered here that little of the original meaning seems to have survived. This remains the case even if individual features such as the complex Janus heads can also be traced back to Mesopotamian prototypes (*cf* Frankfort 1970, Pl 136). Attempts to link the main figure with the story of Gilgamesh, with Indo-Iranian, Vedic and Zoroastrian religions are conjectural. Assyria, which was the major power of the time, exercised negligible artistic influence on these, as on other Luristan bronzes. Only the *polos*, or headdress, of **62** is reminiscent of Assyrian kings' headdresses (*cf* Hrouda 1965, Pl 50).

Prior to recent scientific excavations, the standards were variously dated to the second or first millennia BC and only after 1930 were they regularly ascribed to the area of Luristan in Iran. Now we have examples associated with pottery of the 8th–7th centuries BC, though of course the standards may have been antiques at the time of deposition. The most informative context is Tomb 4 at Tattulban where one like **61** lay beside the head of a single interment (Vanden Berghe 1968, 125–7, Figs 45, 46.6). The body was richly equipped with iron dagger, quiver, arrows and shield; the last two were indicated by a metal boss and seven arrowheads respectively. Standards therefore were part of the burial rituals of warriors and consequently the 'Master-of-Animals' theme also had mortuary connotations. However, as Muscarella points out (1988a, 36–9), only one of some 400 carefully excavated tombs has yielded a standard and so they were probably used in other settings (*cf* the 8th–7th centuries temple context on Samos) or Tuttulban might be outside the area where they were more commonly interred with the dead.

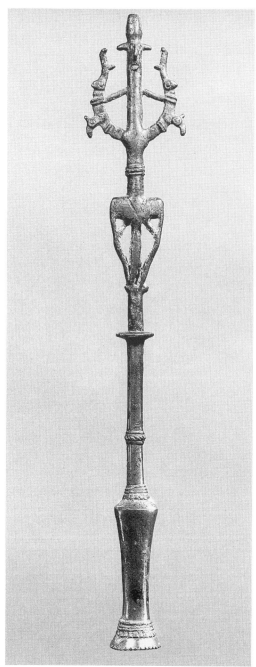

61

62

63

64

61 Standard 33.180

c 850–650 BC. Unprovenanced, probably from Luristan, Western Iran.
Hollow, complete 'standard' with, at top, a Janus-headed figure grasping opposed, open mouthed animals arranged in an arc with hoopoes' heads projecting outwards between the figure's hands and central stem. Animal hind quarters and elongated legs project below this and a ribbed ridge. This element of the standard is slotted into a socket in a bottle-shaped mount with upper flange and notched rib near an elaborate, expanded, concave stand framed by a series of plain and notched fillets. The finial is of different composition from the mount and perhaps suspect (see Appendix A). Cast *bronze*.
Height 0.384 m   Width (upper animals) 0.064 m
McLellan Galleries 12, left ill; Exh. Glasgow 1949, No 685.
Acquired W. Williams, 1948.

62 Part Of A Standard 33.89

c 850–650 BC. Unprovenanced, probably from Luristan, Western Iran.
Upper part of a hollow standard with a Janus-headed figure and opposed snarling beasts, the bodies of which form an arc. The central figure wears a cylindrical *polos* with upper ridge terminal. It has large circular eyes, small breasts and fist-like feet indicated at the juncture of the central stem and animals arc. Below are four ribs on the stem, two projecting animal hindquarters and elongated angular legs that extend down to the concave-sided pedestal 'base'. Cast *bronze*.
Height 0.182 m   Width 0.058 m
Unpublished. Exh. Glasgow 1949, No 681.
Acquired M. Hakim, 1946.

63 Part Of A Standard 33.88

c 850–650 BC. Unprovenanced, probably from Luristan, Western Iran.
Hollow rod with, at the top, a Janus-headed figure with two snarling beasts forming an arc, their noses touching his elongated ears. The central figure wears a biconical headdress and there is a triple ridged projection at the juncture of the animal arc and the main stem. Below a double ring are the projecting

hindquarters of animals with bowed legs rejoining the stem at small loops near the base. Cast *bronze*.
Height 0.148 m   Width 0.07 m
Unpublished. Exh. Glasgow 1949, No 692.
Acquired M. Hakim, 1947.

64 Part Of A Standard 33.90

c 850–650 BC. Unprovenanced, probably from Luristan, Western Iran.
Top of hollow standard with Janus-headed figure between fantastic beasts forming an arc. The central figure has a biconical headdress, elongated facial features outlined by a V-shaped ridge, exaggerated crescent-shaped ears, two rings below the head and, at the juncture with the arc, a circular boss inside a V-shaped relief band. The figure's arms are bent awkwardly at the elbows and it holds beasts with crests above their large eyes; hoopoes' (?) heads stem from the back of their necks near the juncture with the central stem. Below a triple ring is part of another, fragmentary beast with attached head or bird(?). Cast *bronze*.
Height 0.121 m   Width 0.073 m
Unpublished. Exh. Glasgow 1949, No 667.
Acquired M. Hakim, 1947.

65 Anthropomorphic Tube 33.92

c 850–650 BC. Unprovenanced, probably from Luristan, Western Iran.
Hollow rod with flounces near its base, ribbed along most of its length and at top, two Janus heads with floral headdress. Cast *bronze*.
Height 0.113 m   Width 0.026 m
Moorey 1971, 165 referring here as elsewhere to 'Glasgow'. Exh. Glasgow 1949, No 697.
Acquired M. Hakim, 1947.

Stylistic similarities between the Janus heads of this tube and those on the standards (**61–4**) strongly suggest that they belong to the same metal-working tradition. For these stylistic reasons therefore the tube is likely to come from Luristan and belong to the late 9th–7th centuries BC (*cf* Moorey 1971, 164). It is one of a well known series of tubes which, because they are hollow like the standards, may have been used in a similar manner. There are other tubes with zoomorphic terminals, so the overt similarity between the Janus head here and that of the Master of Animals on the standards points to a kindred symbolism.

The top of another tube was found in the Level IIA 'Fort' at Baba Jan, a site with, according to its excavator, C. Goff, a Median Fort and Manor (1978, 38, Fig 14.26). Leaving aside the questionable attribution of the site to Medians, uncertainty attaches to the proposed context of the object and its consequent 7th century BC date. Muscarella has pointed to the excavator's own admission that workmen may have introduced a Luristan pin to the site during excavations (1988b, 140 n.1); hence there is a risk that this too was planted. In fact, Baba Jan which was probably an important Luristan centre, produced surprisingly few bronzes. This may be due to pillage consequent upon its destruction, but it only serves to emphasize the exasperating contrast between the multitude of bronzes derived from clandestine operations and the dearth from controlled fieldwork.

66 Figure Attachment 33.85

c 1000–500 BC. Unprovenanced, probably from Kurdistan, Western Iran.
Column-shaped figure with separately indicated feet, arms raised up, schematised face with 'Hathor' braids and small horns. Below the horns on the plain reverse is a loop. Cast *bronze*.
Height 0.112 m   Width 0.08 m
Unpublished. Exh. Glasgow 1949, No 683.
Acquired F. Partridge, 1948.

Many of these attachment figures were found in clandestine excavations near Piravend in Kurdistan (Moorey 1971, 168). The styles vary considerably, with plaque, or as here, columnar bodies predominating (*cf* Hôtel Drouot 1972, 210). The robust loops suggest that these schematised figures were meant to withstand hard wear, perhaps when fixed to horse harness.

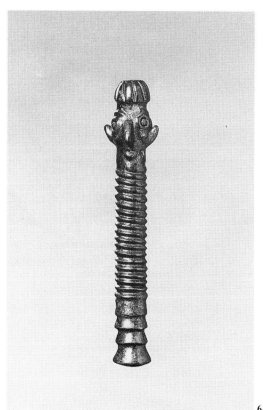

65

66

67 Zoomorphic Figurine 28.76

(?) 2nd–1st millennia BC. Unprovenanced,
possibly from Western Iran.

Standing bull (?) with, straight splayed legs, thin
cylindrical body and small flat-nosed head. Only
one, small horn survives intact and the projecting
ears are placed between the bases of the horns and
the large eyes, applied as circular pellets. A ridge
extends along its upright neck; the shoulders and
boney haunches are differentiated from the body. A
rectangular projection rises from the back above the
haunches: this may be incomplete with a small
socket (? intentional). The short tail extends unnaturally from this projection. No sex is indicated
and the cleft of the hooves is barely incised. Cast
bronze.

Height 0.078 m   Length 0.092 m
Unpublished.
Acquired K.G. Hewett, 1955.

Standing bronze animal figures from Luristan
are particularly common. They are usually
pierced or stylised with a loop between the neck
and the back so that they could be hung as
pendants. The stylisation of this one renders a
west Iranian origin possible (*cf* the somewhat
smaller bull in Hôtel Drouot 1973, Pl XIV.151).

Pins of many varieties are also typical of Luristan bronzes. Several, including elaborate types like **69**, were found in the walls of the 8–7th century temple at Surkh Dum in eastern Luristan where they may have been used as votives or icons rather than garment pins (Muscarella 1981b, 336; 1988b, 124–6). They were also deposited in burials, as in Bard-i Bal grave **68**, dated to the first quarter of the 1st millennium BC, where the pin presumably acted as a dress fastener (Vanden Berghe 1971, 21, Fig 18). Since the same floral-headed type was deposited in such different places, it fulfilled a number of functions. Far more contextual information than is presently available will be needed to elucidate the significance of these multi-purpose pins therefore.

Types include pins with large openwork and solid terminals, as well as simpler examples. The former group usually depicts elaborate figurative themes familiar from the standards. One variant series, sometimes referred to as 'wands', has distinctive square terminals. The Master of Animals here often possesses horns and hair curls like those on the Piravend figures (**66**). He is typically depicted holding animals with spiral attachments (**68**). In naturalistically rendered bodies the female form, sometimes in birthing posture, is clear and so some of the 'masters' may in fact be 'mistresses'. It has been suggested that the solid disc **70** imitates rush fans of the kind that appear on decorated situlae (Moorey 1971, 215). The remaining pin-head could have been a stylized poppy. An identical one exists in the Ashmolean Museum (1951.267).

Frequently the shanks of these pins were made of iron which by rusting become detached from the bronze terminal.

68   Decorated Pin With Case   33.181

c 1000–700 BC. Unprovenanced, probably from Luristan, Western Iran.

Pin with shank wrapped in its case comprised of a piece of plain, folded bronze. Its openwork terminal consists of a columnar, horned figure grasping inverted ibexes(?) whose hindquarters are attached to the encircling frame of snarling beasts by spirals. Between this frame and the pin shaft are simple volutes and incised ribs. Cast *bronze*.

Height 0.222 m   Width 0.007 m

Hannah 1953, 350.11; Moorey 1971, 205.

Acquired A. Garabed, 1952.

69 Decorated Pin Terminal 33.105

c 1000–600 BC. Unprovenanced, probably
from Luristan, Western Iran.

Inside a square frame with herring-bone pattern, a
columnar, human-headed figure is grasped on either
side by rampant felines. A ribbed socket for the lost
pin shank projects from the border below the figure.
Cast *bronze* with tin-enriched surface (see Appendix
A).

Height 0.078 m   Width 0.06 m
Marks 1983, 29, Fig 7; Exh. Glasgow 1949, No 691.
Acquired F. Partridge, 1948.

**70 Terminal Of Disc-Headed
Pin** 33.108

c 1000–600 BC. Unprovenanced, probably
from Luristan, Western Iran.

Detached top of a disc-headed pin with four concentric bands of dots and squares around a central
boss. Top of shank still addheres. Cast *bronze* pin
with *iron* shank.

Height 0.054 m   Width 0.038 m
Unpublished.
Acquired A. Garabed, 1948.

71 Floral-Headed Pin 33.94

c 1000–600 BC. Unprovenanced, probably
from Luristan, Western Iran.

Slightly bent and broken shank with three incised
ribs under its head, a knobbed oval terminal with
four bosses, each with a socket and one with incised
rays around the socket. Slightly encrusted cast
bronze.

Length 0.164 m   Width 0.017 m
Unpublished.
Acquired M. Hakim, 1947.

Neo-Assyrian records repeatedly refer to horses in lands on their eastern borders, but few excavated specimens, like those in 'royal' burials in Cyprus, have been recovered. The several that in their panic became trapped in the destruction of Level IV at Hasanlu unfortunately appear not to have been harnessed. Explicit archaeological evidence therefore largely comes from depictions and isolated harness elements, in particular the sturdy bits and exuberantly designed cheek–pieces.

While the earliest metal horsebits come from 16th–15th centuries Palestine and 14th century BC Amarna in Egypt, it was in Luristan that these were first regularly transformed into expressions of applied art. Metal-workers employed animal motifs, both real and fantastic, for the cheek-pieces. This is shown in the stylized moufflon of **74** and the griffin of **73**. The latter were borrowed from Mesopotamian iconography, perhaps through Elam, and it was there and in Luristan itself that the motif was modified to suit local expression. More realistic are the horses or asses on **72**. Here a certain breed may have been intended (Moorey 1971, 114–20) and there is a further note of realism in the bells slung round their necks. Such bells are shown in an identical position on a cylinder seal (Fig 22) from Necropolis B at Tepe Sialk, as well as on a relief of the Assyrian king Tiglath-pileser III (744–727 BC) (Boehmer 1965, 803–10). They have also been found in Luristan in association with horse harness equipment (see **77**). As is usually the case with Luristan bronzes, there is almost a total absence of reliable information concerning the contexts of cheek-pieces. Some examples are reported from controlled excavations, but details are scanty (Muscarella 1988b, 36).

The question of whether these were for real or only funerary use has long been debated. Many show signs of wear and the goads and loops on interiors are functionally designed. There is equivocal evidence for horse burials in Iran (Moorey 1971, 103) and figurative examples like **73** were depicted in use by cavalrymen on Assyrian reliefs of the time of Sennacherib (704–681 BC) (Fig 23). Assyria looked to the east for horses and horsemanship; this is an instance of influence on equestrian harness equipment from regions where it was more highly developed. An example of bronze or electrum (?) was discovered at Nimrud (Mallowan 1966, 128, Fig 70) and both it and the reliefs show that the Assyrians adapted the idea, perhaps as a consequence of Sennacherib's raid into remote Luristan in 702 BC. The Assyrian cheekpieces lack the base line common to all Luristan examples and so if Lur horses were taken to Assyria, they were kitted out with local harness equipment.

22 Impression of cylinder seal from Tepe Sialk, Iran (*after* Boehmer 1965, 805, Fig 1b).

23 Detail of relief of Sennacherib showing use of zoo-morphic horsebit (*after* Porada 1965, 85, Pl 21 below)

72 Figured Cheek-Pieces And Bit 33.111

c 1000–600 BC. Unprovenanced, probably
from Luristan, Western Iran.
On the rectangular, sectioned bit, with terminals
curled in opposite directions, are two sliding cheek-
pieces cast as horses and executed in *ajouré* on a
base line. Only their obverses are modelled with
small donkey-like heads, ears pricked forward,
manes, a sash with bells round the necks, flat bodies
with sharply defined haunches, male genitalia and
long tails attached to the base of the hind leg and
encircled by a ribbon(?). Reverses have two projecting teeth and two loops. Slight projections under
the base bar, below each animal hoof. Cast *bronze*.
Length of bar 0.147 m   Height 0.083 m
Unpublished. Exh. Glasgow 1949, No 683.
Acquired A. Garabed, 1948.

73 Figured Cheek-Pieces And Bit 33.106

c 1000–600 BC. Unprovenanced, probably
from Luristan, Western Iran.
On the square-sectioned bar with terminals coiled in
opposite directions are two sliding, animal cheek-
pieces. Each is composed of flat, conjoined and abbreviated griffins with top knots, and necks embellished with ruffs and curls. Bodies are not indicated
and loops are placed behind the ears. The plain
reverses have six projecting teeth. Several curls and
other details are missing. Cast *bronze*.
Length of bar 0.216 m   Height 0.09 m
Moorey 1971, 123. Exh. Glasgow 1949, No 688.
Acquired A. Garabed, 1948.

74 Figured Cheek-Pieces 33.178/9

c 1000–600 BC. Unprovenanced, probably
from Luristan, Western Iran.
A pair of cheek-pieces composed of conjoined
moufflons worked in *ajouré* on a bar base-line. The
hole for the bar is in the centre of the conjoined
bodies which face in opposing directions, with heads
regardant. The narrow muzzles are on long necks,
large curled horns almost touch. Knobs (incipient
curls?) occur on legs and the bodies are V-shaped.
Reverses have two projecting teeth and two loops.
Some details missing. Cast *bronze*.
Height 0.13 m   Width 0.123 m
McLellan Galleries 13; Exh. Glasgow 1949, No 678
& 680.
Acquired M. Hakim, 1945.

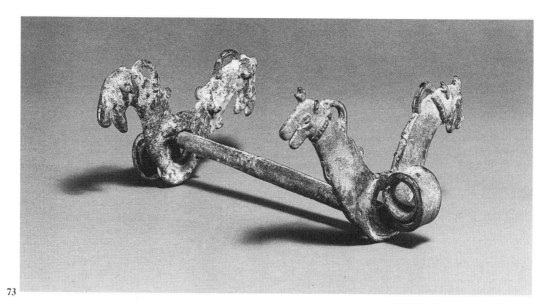

73

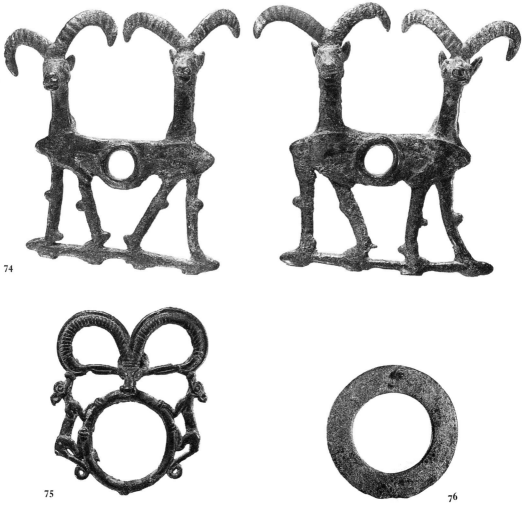

74

75

76

75 Harness Ring 33.177

c 800–600 B C. Unprovenanced, probably from Luristan, Western Iran.

Stereotyped design of two felines biting the large horns of a moufflon head, the entire group set on a circular ring. The exaggerated sweep of horns is set on the same, flat plane as the circle, their tips touching elongated ears. The reverse is plain, encrusted, with a loop behind the moufflon head. Cast *bronze*.

Height 0.097 m   Width 0.076 m
Unpublished.
Acquired F. Partridge, 1948.

76 Harness Ring 33.93

c 800–600 B C. Unprovenanced, probably from Luristan, Western Iran.

Annular, flat ring of cast *bronze*, thickest on interior, narrowing to outer edge. Traces of radial wear marks or fabric impression on one side.

Diameter 0.047 m
Unpublished.
Acquired M. Hakim, 1946.

The flamboyantly decorated ring **75** was most probably used in horse harnessing (*cf* Moorey 1971, 130), but its delicacy suggests that it was not intended for daily use. On the other hand, the simple ring, **76**, is heavy and the radial striations indicate that it saw considerable use, presumably in conjunction with cross-straps. Such plain rings are likely to have been employed increasingly with the growth of cavalry in the Assyrian army during the 7th century B C. There are few published parallels however and most of these are from Luristan. Perhaps the most informative context is tomb 150 at War Kabud where Vanden Berghe seems to have found a large part of an equestrian harness outfit, even though there were no traces of an equid present (1987, 262, Fig 16.6–7). Together with two rings of this type were bridle bits, snaffle, three bells, buttons and five 'phaleres'. It is not known what position these sturdy rings occupied within the harness equipment. They are quite distinct from the common penannular rings with circular sections which most likely were bracelets or anklets (Moorey 1971, Pl 64).

77 Bracelet 33.176

c 1000–500 B C. Unprovenanced, probably from Luristan, Western Asia.

Rectangular sectioned bracelet with two engraved lines and a hatched lattice pattern near the animal terminals. These have protruding eyes and a long, flat-ended muzzle with herring-bone design and lines indicating a mouth. Cast *bronze*.

Diameter 0.069 m   Average Width 0.008 m
Hannah 1956, 186.11 Exh. Glasgow 1949, No 689.
Acquired M. Hakim, 1948.

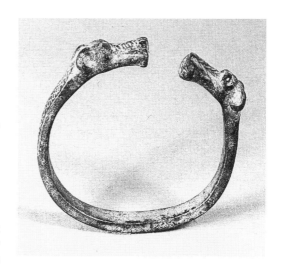

78 Whetstone With Wild Goat Handle 33.211

c 1100–900 B C. Unprovenanced, probably from Luristan, Western Iran.

Whetstone in socketed handle with wild goat terminal. The tubular handle has two tenon holes, but these are empty now. Its terminal is shaped as a kneeling goat with an elongated, arched neck and two horns sweeping in large curves back to the neck, each with eight encircling bars. Strengthening joints are inserted once between the horns and from the goat's chin to its neck. Cast *bronze* handle.

Length of holder 0.166 m   Height 0.089 m   Total Length 0.295 m
Wells 1958a, 438.5, Fig 5.
Acquired F. Partridge, 1956.

79 Wild Goat Handle   33.209

c 1100–900 B C. Unprovenanced, probably
from Luristan, Western Iran.

The hollow body of this wild goat-headed sleeve
still contains part of a whetstone, unfastened,
although tenon holes exist. The terminal of the
sleeve is shaped as a recumbent, bearded goat with
arched neck and heavy horns looped back to the
neck, each horn with four straps on their external
face. Its ears are in relief, eyes and mouth incised.
Cast *bronze*.

Length 0.086 m   Height 0.06 m
Wells 1958a, 164. 58, Fig 2.
Acquired Spink & Son, 1955.

Several, almost identical, whetstones are known
from Luristan. They demonstrate the continued
necessity to sharpen bronze and, by their
numbers, the large amount of bronze that must
have circulated in that area; also, the highland
inclination to decorate even the most utilitarian
tools with stylised animals (Moorey 1971, 98–
100). They were placed as grave goods in such

cist tombs as Bard-i-Bal 2, 67 and 68 dated to
c 1250–1000 B C (Vanden Berghe 1970, 354–7,
Figs 117.8, 119; 1972a, 129–30, Figs 36.12, 37A,
37B). The date range of these tombs is significant
since it establishes that later features of Luristan
metalwork such as 'animal art' began by at least
the later second millennium B C.

80 Pick Head   33.104

c 2600–1800 B C. Unprovenanced, from
Luristan, Western Iran(?).

Shaft-hole pick with short cylindrical shaft, cut
away at its base and continued downwards opposite
the blade. The shaft rims are strengthened by triple
relief bands, and a large flange with medial rib
extends opposite the blade. It is nearly square in
section, tapering and with slight ribs on the upper
and lower sides. Cast arsenical *bronze*, encrusted.

Height 0.082 m   Length 0.176 m
Unpublished.
Acquired F. Partridge, 1948.

This specialized type of weapon enjoyed widespread use, from Iran to North Syria, in the
second half of the third and the early second
millennium B C. It is thus much earlier than
the more ornate pieces of metalwork described in
other parts of this catalogue. Few other weapons
have such an enormous spatial distribution at
this time and its exceptional status, at least in
Sumer and Akkad, is borne out by its incorporation as a major filling motif in a dramatic combat
scene on an Akkadian cylinder seal (Fig 25).
Precious stones such as lapis lazuli and the rare
metal, tin, came from the east to these regions of

79

Western Asia now and so it may be linked in some manner to this prestige trade. It follows therefore that the pick head need not have been found in western Iran, though the type was undoubtedly popular there (Calmeyer 1969, 33–6; Moorey 1971, 63. 32).

Although Luristan does not lie on the main east-west communication routes, many examples allegedly from western Iran probably come from that region. One example was buried in a single inhumation grave at Kalleh Nisar which Vanden Berghe dates *c* 2400–2100 BC (1969, 280 top). The site consists of a cemetery divided into at least two sections, one with immensely long stone lined pits for communal burials, the other with small pits for single inhumations. Analysis may eventually determine if there are social as well as chronological reasons for this division.

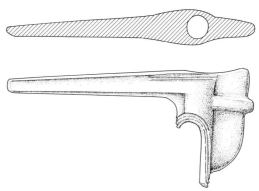

24   Pick head 80.

80

Axe-heads have a long history in western Iran. A tendency to lengthen the blade and to embellish the butt occurred in the late second – early first millennium B C (Moorey 1971, 39–71). Thus the relatively plain example **81** could be early in the series and it belongs to a type that developed from late 3rd millennium Sumerian precursors. Its distribution lies in South Mesopotamia and southwest Iran, the latter yielding an example inscribed with the name of the Elamite King, Untash-GAL, *c* 1250 B C (Ghirshman 1966, Pl 53.3). Others like **82** bear inscriptions of the 12th century B C. These two features, the occurrence of inscribed axe-heads and the occurrence of examples beyond Luristan in Elam and Babylonia, distinguish this early group from the somewhat later 'Luristan' bronzes that comprise most of the ancient Asiatic metalwork in the Burrell Collection. Different political circumstances pertained at that earlier period and it is likely that relations with Elam were closer and that Late Kassite involvement in these areas of western Iran were intense.

Further dating evidence for these weapons has also been forthcoming from excavations. Thus, spike-butted axe-heads like **84** have been found together with independently dated grave goods in tomb 2 at Bard-i Bal (Vanden Berghe 1970, 354–6, Figs 117.5, 120). Another like **82** comes from the exceptionally rich tomb A10 at Kutal-i Gulgul which had some 38 pots, a spearhead and other objects associated with more than one interment (Vanden Berghe 1973, 22 top, 24.50). Both graves are to be assigned to the late second millennium, *c* 1200–1000 B C.

While these axe-heads demonstrate that metal-working traditions characterised by a love of elaboration and figurative decoration flourished in Luristan in the later second millennium, well before the *floruit* of the industry, they also reveal something of the motivation for the creation of that industry. It is clear from the exceedingly sloped angles of the blades of **82**, **83** and especially **84** that they could hardly be intended for functional purposes. Their deposition in graves, as well as in a sacred setting in Elam (and perhaps a spike-butted(?) antique at Surkh Dum), indicates that they were primarily intended for burial and ceremony. They were rare in Elam where they may have been reserved for the highest echelons of society. In Luristan however they occur in tombs of varied richness and perhaps ownership status. Other mechanisms for the dissemination of such ornate goods through society must therefore have obtained in these Highland regions.

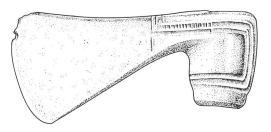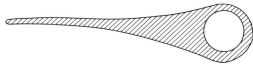

26 Socketed axe head 81.

81 Socketed Axe Head 33.109

c 1300–800 B C. Unprovenanced, probably from Luristan, Western Iran.
Shaft-hole axe, cylindrical socket with three ridges near the base, up the side opposite the blade and extending along the rim and slightly onto the blade: The middle ridge is hatched, but this is considerably worn. The lobate blade expands to a slightly convex edge; rims are thickened. Chipped cutting edge. Cast *bronze*.
Height 0.056 m   Length 0.151 m
Unpublished.
Acquired A. Garabed, 1948.

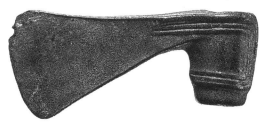

83 Socketed Axe Head 33.102

c 1300–800 B C. Unprovenanced, probably from Luristan, Western Iran.
Shaft-hole axe with short, cylindrical socket composed of four joined ridges which project opposite the blade where they leave three eyes. The blade is angled downwards with a straight upper rim and concave lower rim, each thickened; the cutting edge is straight. Encrusted, cast *bronze*.
Height 0.077 m   Length 0.201 m
Unpublished.
Acquired F. Partridge, 1948.

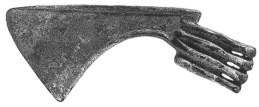

82 Socketed Axe Head 33.103

c 1300–800 B C. Unprovenanced, probably from Luristan, Western Iran.
Shaft-hole axe, short cylindrical socket with four ridges composed of triple relief bands which extend opposite the blade into animal heads with flat, joined snouts as terminals; only the top two heads have an intermediate strengthening rib. The blade emerges from the jaws of a lion's head modelled partly on the socket. It has thickened rims, the upper horizontal, the lower concave. Straight, slightly downward facing cutting edge. Cast *bronze*.
Height 0.078 m   Length 0.20 m
Unpublished.
Acquired F. Partridge, 1948.

84 Socketed Axe Head 33.190

c 1300–800 B C. Unprovenanced, probably from Luristan, Western Iran.
Shaft-hole axe, tapered cylindrical socket with four long spikes projecting opposite the blade. Each spike is continued as a slight ridge round the haft, the lowest as a rim for its base, the next looped over it to continue as the lower rim of the blade, the next as a short medial rib onto the blade and the topmost as the upper flange of the blade. This blade expands to a downward-facing, straight cutting edge, its lower rim forming an incomplete elongated oval with the shaft. Cast *bronze*.
Height 0.067 m   Length 0.217 m
Unpublished.
Acquired Spink & Son, 1950.

85 Macehead 33.112

c 2300–2000 BC. Unprovenanced, probably
from Iran or Mesopotamia.

Tapered cylindrical macehead with, closer to its
wider end, a globular body with three rows of
vertical ridge studs. The body is bordered by two
moulds, rims are everted. Cast *bronze* with a slight
patina and one minor hole.

Height 0.099 m   Diameter 0.078 m
Unpublished.

Acquired A. Garabed, 1948.

Maceheads of metal first occur in the 4th millennium BC in the Near East. Long sleeved types
with vertical, continuous ribs are known from
the time of King Naram-Sin of Akkad (*c* 2254–
2218 BC) (Calmeyer 1969, 26, Fig 24). Subsequently, sleeves become shorter and facets or
spikes are more varied, and, still in the later 3rd
millennium BC, at Tepe Hissar in Iran and at
Ashur in Iraq, maceheads with the shorter sleeve
and ridge studs make their appearance. They are
not common and the stratified example from
Ashur is a particularly close parallel (*ibid* 119). It
has the same elongated sleeve above the globular
body with two rows of ridge studs and border of
double mouldings, and a less pronounced flare to
the sleeve below.

This macehead belongs to a time when, in
general, such objects were passing out of use as
functional battlefield weapons. Indeed, they may
always have had a more symbolic role in urban
societies which possessed large corps of
spearmen. Thus, on the Stele of the Vultures
from Tello-Girsu (*c* 2450 BC) it is the god
Ningirsu, not the king with his army, who wields
a mace (Strommenger & Hirmer 1969, Pls 66–9).
Inscribed examples from Mesopotamia divulge
that from Sumerian to Assyrian times maces
were a sign of royalty and a symbol of authority.
They were used especially in rituals, as divine
emblems, put on display during judicial disputes
and offered to deities as votives (Cocquerillat
1952). The Burrell macehead is unprovenanced
however and so it could have come from another
kind of society in which it may well have served
other purposes. There was a resurgence in the
manufacture of metal maceheads with rows of
blunt and sharp spikes in the earlier first millennium BC in various parts of the Near East, including for the first time such western locations
as Cyprus (*SCE* IV.2, 141, Fig 24.11; Muscarella
1988b, 57—8).

86 Flange-Hilted Dagger 33.97

c 1300–900 BC. Unprovenanced, possibly
from Western Iran.

Narrow bladed dagger cast in one with the handle,
originally inlaid. Straight-sided, flanged hilt narrowing to splayed, convex pommel, no shoulders.
Tapered blade, hexagonal in section, tapering
medial ridges. Chipped. Cast *bronze.*

Length 0.351 m   Width 0.031 m
Unpublished.

Acquired M. Hakim, 1947.

Flange-hilted daggers came into circulation in
the first half of the second millennium BC in
the Levant and thereafter enjoyed widespread
popularity throughout the Near East, from
Oman to Palestine (Curtis 1983, 75–6; Muscarella 1988b, 54–5). Slight morphological differences help in dating and in the definition of
contemporary regional variants. Thus, during
the period when this example is likely to have
been manufactured, Levantine daggers have
much deeper flanges while others in the Persian

Gulf region differ yet again (Yon 1987, 364–7). The closest analogies for this Burrell dagger are found in Luristan (Moorey 1971, 71–2) and although there can be no certainty, this is a likely origin.

As in the case of decorated axe-heads like **82**, several daggers of this type carry at the top of their blades inscriptions of Babylonian kings of the end of the second millennium BC such as Marduk-nādin-aḫḫe (*c* 1110–1082 BC). Basing his conclusions on the inscriptional evidence, Calmeyer places the type between 1250 and 1050 BC (1969, 60). More recent evidence suggests that it persisted into the 10th century (Vanden Berghe 1972b, 44–8, Fig 11.37–8, Pl 20.1: two examples from a tomb at Shurabah) and perhaps the 9th century BC (Moorey 1971, 71). It may have continued in use even later in Oman (Lombard 1981).

Vanden Berghe supposes that an almost identical example from Bard-i Bal tomb 2 had an inlay of wood or other material secured to the handle by flanges bent over near the base of the hilt (1970, 354–5, Figs 117.4, 5, 118c). Such lappets may originally have existed on this dagger which also no doubt had an inlay of perishable or precious material. Related types with bifurcated pommels retain stone and gold-sheathed wood inlays (Muscarella 1988b, 286–7).

Tomb 2 at Bard-i Bal is instructive insofar as this dagger and a number of the other Burrell Luristan bronzes are paralleled in its funerary furniture. Thus there were two flange-hilted daggers, an axe similar to **84** and a whetstone like **78**. The warrior was also accompanied by three pots and two bronze vessels. Although richer than many graves, it is not outstanding and it provides some idea of the wealth of Highland warriors, their burial armaments and the kind of graves such objects were once placed in. The extraordinarily rich tomb A–10 at Kutal-i Gulgul contained four daggers of this type (Vanden Berghe 1973).

87 Spouted Libation Beaker 33.215

Iranian or Sumerian; *c* 2500–2000 B C.
Unprovenanced. Said to be from "Persia,
Luristan".

Tall, slender beaker with straight-sided body expanding from splayed, hollow base to flat rim. A
narrow, pinched spout extends from near the base
in a long curve outwards to the level of the rim.
Both basal and rim lips have been folded over, with,
at one side of the spout, a small repair (?) clamp *in
situ* over the rim. A secondary hole beneath the rim
and almost opposite the spout has been punched
from the inside. Made of sheet *silver*, its well
preserved surface has an iridescent, mottled appearance, the latter a result of hammering. Complete,
with minor indents and a crack.

Height 0.178 m   Diameter 0.129 m

Wells 1958a, 438.1.

Acquired Spink & Son, 1957.

Tall, slender goblets in such precious materials
as this are very rare in the Ancient Near East.
Parallels were found in the 'royal' cemetery at Ur
(Woolley 1934, Pl 235. 42–3) but they lack the
pronounced, elegant spout of this example. So
too does the otherwise similar goblet, also in
silver, which is held by a bull figure and ascribed
by Hansen to the Proto-Elamite Period of South
West Iran (1970, 6, Fig 1). When bronze vessels
of the 3rd millennium B C from Susa and
Luristan possess such exaggerated spouts, their
bodies do not conform to this sophisticated
shape. A late 3rd millennium B C bronze goblet
from Tello-Girsu however is closer to this silver
goblet in many details (Nagel 1963, 42, Pl
LXXV. 1–6 for this and others) and its existence
warrants consideration of vessels of different
materials from that site.

Executed in steatite, a royal libation beaker of
King Gudea of Lagash (*c* 2200 B C) dedicated
to the god Ningizzida is embellished with a pair
of Mushhush dragons and twining snakes on its
long narrow spout (Fig 28). Stripped of this
relief decoration, it is clear that the beaker has
virtually the same shape as, though slightly
larger (H 0.23, D 0.12 m) than, the Burrell
vessel. With its concave spout, the silver beaker
has a more graceful line than the lapidary could

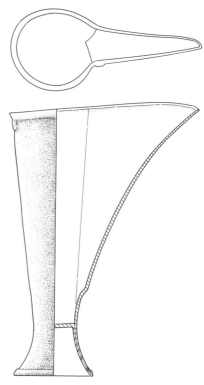

27   Spouted libation beaker **87**.

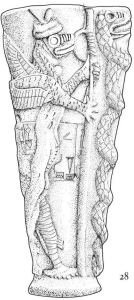

29 Detail of wall painting in the Audience Chamber of the palace at Mari showing king with libation beaker (*after* Parrot 1958, Pl XVII).

28 Spouted libation beaker of Gudea (*after* Moortgat 1969, Pl 187).

manage for Gudea's beaker and so the latter is likely to be a copy of metal prototypes. Support for this suggestion is forthcoming from Braun-Holzinger's proposal that the type is to be identified with the signs 'REC 447a LA' which appear on the spout of another fragmentary steatite example from Tello (Braun-Holzinger 1989). According to related inscriptional evidence, this type of vessel was often made of silver, gold, bronze and lapis lazuli in late Sumerian times. In other words, its shape was primarily fashioned in metal. King Ibbi-Suen of Ur (*c* 2028–2004 BC), amongst others, dedicated one of these metal beakers to the gods, hence they are associated with royalty and were intended as cultic equipment.

Extant vessels and representations provide further information on the use and dating of these rare, prestige items. Earlier and partly contemporary libation vessels in Mesopotamia are normally supplied with a tubular spout (e.g. Fig 7; Parrot 1948, 88–90, Fig 22b; Woolley 1934, 282, Pl 102b; and on Enheduanna's disc: Moortgat 1969, Pl 130). Elegantly tapered vessels with pronounced spouts, and sometimes a foot, appear in pictorial art at least from the Akkadian Period. A possible earlier example, carried by an attendant on Eannatum's votive macehead, is too indistinct to be certain (Strommenger & Hirmer 1964, Pl 70). In all instances

such vessels are used for libations in presentation scenes. Thus on a seal in the Morgan Library a man holding a goat pours a libation from such a beaker into a large container(?) at the foot of a seated deity (Winter 1986, Pl 62.1). In another seal of the Akkadian Period, the beaker is held by the seated deity (Moortgat 1940, Pl 27.192). On the obverse of his stele, the rather later King Ur-Nammu (*c* 2112–2095 BC) used a similar vessel, perhaps with abbreviated spout, to decant liquid into plant-pots situated on the platform beside seated deities (*ibid* Pl 63; *Brussels* 57.111). This ritual is repeated on a wall-painting in the Audience Chamber of the Palace at Mari. There the king in a flounced robe pours liquid into two yellow (=gold?) pedestal vessels from a tall, flared beaker (Fig 29). A fine stone example, perhaps without spout, was found in the same palace (Parrot 1967, Pl 72.2216).

In his study of the Mari painting, Moortgat noted the similarity of the king's beaker to Gudea's and he dated the painting a little later than the reign of that ruler on stylistic grounds (1969, 73). The exact date of Gudea is disputed, but in any case the painting was still visible at the time of the destruction of the palace at Mari by Hammurabi in his 33rd year, *c* 1760 BC. That such beakers were still in use in the earlier part of the second millennium BC is also suggested by its appearance in a similar composition on an

Old Babylonian terracotta relief plaque from Isin (Hrouda 1977, Pl 23. 1B39).

This beaker therefore may be a uniquely preserved instance of a highly prestigious, perhaps royal, libation vessel of the late third – early second millennium BC, of a type usually preserved in stone. Silver had been used for vessels in Mesopotamia previously, for example a libation vessel and ewer from the 'royal' cemetery at Ur (Woolley 1934, Pls 171–2), but these are rare. With the decline in the practice of depositing metal vessels towards the end of the third millennium BC in Sumer, metal examples are known exclusively from textual evidence. As Braun-Holzinger (1989) notes, the recorded weight of such 'REC 447a La' beakers is mainly from 400 to 600 g, rather more than our example which weights 222.5 g. Silver vessels in pre-Achaemenid western Iran are also very rare. Its alleged Luristan provenance is not impossible however since metal-work with names of kings of the Akkadian Period has been found there (Calmeyer 1969, 161; *cf.* also Amiet 1986, Fig. 73). Such inscribed metalwork confirms that connections between South Mesopotamia and Luristan existed at least during the earlier history of this sacred vessel type.

88 Small Jar 33.110

c 900–700 BC. Unprovenanced, probably from Luristan, Western Iran.

Slightly rounded disc base with carinated and horizontally constricted body, wide concave neck, flat everted rim. Complete except for small holes in body. Thin sheet metal *bronze*.

Height 0.086 m   Diameter 0.092 m

Unpublished.

Acquired A. Garabed, 1948.

This type of jar is one of the most distinctive products of Iron Age Luristan metalworkers; it is also found beyond that area, in Elam and Babylonia (Moorey 1971, 264–6). At Karkhai, Luristan, in the rich tomb 1, it occurs in association with other objects including an imported Neo-Elamite faience pyxis which can be dated with some certainty to the 9th–8th centuries BC (Vanden Berghe 1973, 28; see also Calmeyer 1969, 115–6). The deceased was equipped with a necklace, silver spiral hair rings,

silver-coated iron needles and sets of three iron rings on each wrist and ankle as well as other objects. The jar was placed inside a decorated bronze bowl by her hands, a pairing that duplicates a set from Uruk (Braun-Holzinger 1988, Fig 92. W 14299a–b). This recurrence suggests that the vessels constituted a drinking or washing set for mortuary purposes.

88

89

89 Handleless Flask 28.44

c 900 (?) BC. Unprovenanced, possibly from Western Iran.

Complete flask with pointed base, biconical body, tall concave neck and upright, flat rim composed of a strip of metal set inside the mouth of the flask. Remainder of vase is composed of a single piece of metal decorated with a row of chased Us along its shoulder. Two dents and one small hole; otherwise in good condition. High purity sheet *copper* with evidence of mineralised textile, most likely linen in a plain tabby weave, on its surface.

Height 0.223 m   Diameter 0.13 m

Hannah 1953, 112.5.

Acquired John Hunt, 1951.

Slender flasks with pointed bases and narrow necks first became popular in the Near East in the late second millennium BC. Examples in pottery, and especially glazed pottery, during the Neo-Assyrian Period have profiles that are close matches for this (*cf* Haller 1954, Pl 3 as–ay). These pottery flasks are also found in Western Iran where, during the first half of the first millennium BC, there are decorated flasks in metal (Calmeyer 1965, Pls 6.J2, 7.O3) with button bases and ridged necks with plain rims, but otherwise akin. One of the most diagnostic decorative features of this known Iranian work, the horizontal band of festoons, each incised with two lines (*ibid*, Pls 1–8), is also found on this flask which may, therefore, be connected with such Iranian work, contemporary with the Neo-Assyrian Empire or later (*cf* Pope 1938, IV, Pl 61). Exact parallels are lacking however and bronze handleless flasks with pointed bases were also known in Mesopotamia (Braun-Holzinger 1986 Pl 90.2N 371). Without well-dated, close parallels, it is not possible to be certain of its cultural context or date, although the purity of its copper suggests a much later date than most parallels mentioned above (see Appendix A).

31 Detail of relief of Tiglath-Pileser III with carinated bowl (*after* Hamilton 1966, 5, Fig 5c).

90 Carinated Bowl 33.113

c 750–300 BC. Unprovenanced, possibly from Western Iran.

Flat-based shallow bowl with rounded shoulders and short, flared neck extending into everted rim. Slight central indentation on interior of base. Sheet *bronze* with patina.

Height 0.053 m   Diameter 0.115 m

Unpublished.

Acquired A. Garabed, 1948.

Bowls of this general type are very popular during the Achaemenid Period (e.g. Pope 1938, 273, Fig 65e) when, for example, they are depicted on the Apadana reliefs at Persepolis (Fig. 33). While many were of precious materials and decorated with gadroons and chased floral

90

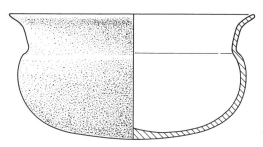

30   Carinated bowl 90.

motifs, plain ones would have been even more common. They occur in fairly ordinary graves, as at Ur (Braun-Holzinger 1988, Fig 91. U. 3366). Most of these however have deeper bodies and taller necks above the carination than our example. They belong to a type which developed concurrently in western Iran and Assyria during the 8th century BC.

Earlier bronze bowls tend to be plain globular types like that at Bard-i Bal tomb 2 which Vanden Berghe dates c 1250–1000 BC (1970, 354, Fig 117.10, 11). By the 8th–7th centuries BC, examples with flat bases, carinations and flared necks have appeared and a number of these are known from Luristan (Van den Berghe 1987, 260, Fig 14.10) and, with decoration, from Assyria (e.g. Mallowan 1966, 116, Pl 59). This type may have emerged somewhat earlier in northwest Iran where at least one prototype has been assigned to the later second millennium BC (Muscarella 1974, 42, Fig 7.2.542), but the Neo-Assyrian evidence shows that it did not gain widespread currency until the 8th century BC.

In Assyrian relief sculptures the type with flat base, shouldered body and short everted rim appears for the first time in the reign of King Tiglath-pileser III (745–727 BC) (Fig 31). Previous examples had plain hemispherical bodies and so the evidence is consistent enough to suggest that our bowl is unlikely to be earlier than the 8th century BC and it may be rather later. Some Assyrian sculptures show that the central indentation in the base was created in order to provide a firm grip when using the bowl for drinking purposes.

91 Amphora With Zoomorphic Handle And Spout 33.214

Achaemenid; 6th–5th centuries BC.
Probably from Massyaf, Syria.
Flat-based amphora, ovoid body, single mould at base of straight expanding neck with slightly everted rim. Two opposed animal handles extend from the shoulder to the rim. One is a bearded goat with the knees of its forelegs poised against the rim, its neck and outward facing head above the rim. Ears and sweeping horns are modelled, eyes, nose, mouth and musculature are engraved and the legs which

continue below the tail in an unbroken curve with the thin body, are traced successfully on one face only. The same traced hair and musculature occur on the bull opposite, rendered in the same posture with brow lines over its swollen eyes and, as the goat, vertical bands of cross-hatching on its neck. It has, in addition, a cut-away spout extending from its back. Complete, with cracked, uneven surface. *Bronze* sheet metal with cast and rivetted handle and spout.

Heavily restored. X-ray examination disclosed several mends with rectangular strips of metal, particularly at the junctures of the handle bases and the body, and patching with organic materials. One of the handles has recently been attached by a screw. There is now no visual evidence for an aperture from the body of the vessel into the hollowed bull-spout, but x-rays suggest this existed originally. See also Appendix A.

Height 0.195 m   Diameter 0.166 m
Amandry 1959, 44–6, Pl 23.1–3; Culican 1965, Pl 51; Wells 1960, 189.1
Acquired Spink & Son, 1957.

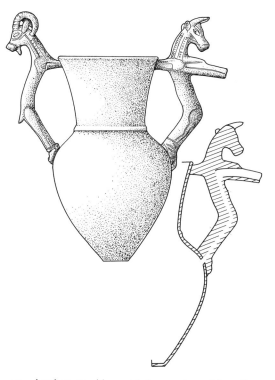

32 Amphora 91 with spout hole reconstructed from X-rays.

A Syrian origin for this impressive display vase, from a hoard found at Massyaf, is to be presumed from antiquity market sources. The 'hoard' was dispersed after its discovery and much of it found its way to the National Museum in Beirut. When he published this amphora in 1959 however, Amandry had seen it in a private collection. He did not doubt its Massyaf origin and he seems to have had detailed information about the circumstances of its recovery since he was able to state that 'le vase était brisé en plusieurs fragments au moment de sa découverte' (1959, 47, n 57). This perhaps explains its present heavily restored condition.

This ornate amphora belongs to a very well known Achaemenid period class, chiefly from its appearance in the hands of various tribute-bearers depicted on the eastern stairway of the Apadana at Persepolis (Fig 33). These sculptures may be attributed to the time of Xerxes (c 485–465 BC) and the amphorae there have plain or gadrooned bodies with zoomorphic handles consisting of winged beasts, one with, the other without a spout as here. They were most probably made of precious metals and later extant amphorae, often surviving only as detached handles, are executed in gold, silver and partially gilded silver. They are much more sophisticated works than this bronze example and they often betray their late date by the inclusion of Hellenistic influences. This amphora lacks all such western traits and as the animal heads appear so archaic, it is to be regarded as one of the earliest examples within the known series of animal-handled amphorae, or a somewhat coarse and archaising provincial work.

33 Detail of Persepolis relief with tribute-bearers carrying bowls and amphorae similar to **90** and **91** (*from* Godard 1965, Pl 48).

While preferring the 7th–6th century BC, Amandry remained uncertain of its date, but for Culican the work is Median, to be dated to c 630 BC (1965, 248.51). There is little supporting evidence for such an early attribution. Its closest parallel is another bronze amphora in the Adam Collection. This has an almost identical body in shape and size, its calf(?) and lion handles are coarsely wrought, their bases are splayed and the lower legs have traced decoration as here. Rivets are used for both ends of the handles instead of simply the lower terminals. Save for the spout, which is replaced by an aperture in the lion to allow the liquid to issue from its mouth, the Adam amphora is executed in the same style as this and should be of similar age. Moorey does not give a date for it and although unprovenanced, it is considered together with other 'Luristan' bronzes (1974, 158–9. 139). As he observes, the addition of a cut-away spout on the Burrell example is typical of the canonical animal-handled amphorae depicted at fifth century BC Persepolis. These constitute the culmination of a long tradition of transforming the handles of luxury metal vessels into animals. Within Iran it was a custom well rooted in Luristan (cf Moorey 1971, Pl 82.522). Beyond this region, the Bubastis silver jug with golden goat handle and other Egyptian finds (e.g. Hayes 1958, 354–8, Figs 221, 224) epitomize the luxurious nature of this cross-cultural and long-lived custom.

The 'hoard' from which the Burrell amphora allegedly comes also contained at least 20 bronze vessels, gold and silver jewellery and other objects, many of which could be dated to the 5th century BC. While there is nothing here that is pre-Achaemenid, this is hardly a convincing way by which to date the amphora; it can now only be done on stylistic grounds and unfortunately, with the lack of well-dated analogies, there are few safe chronological frameworks to apply. We need to know much more about provincial metal production in Achaemenid times and Median and other metal-working centres in pre-Achaemenid times in Iran before this amphora can be attributed to its appropriate historical context with confidence. If it does come from Massyaf, then it is likely to have been deposited there only after the establishment of Persian rule in the west.

92　Lidded Flask　33.213

Achaemenid Period (?). Unprovenanced.
Elongated, ovoid body with knobbed base, long,
cylindrical neck and small convex lid surmounted by
the foreparts of a rampant bull(?). Around the
shoulder an uneven guilloche band bordered by
single rows of relief squares separates dependant
petals above, upright ones below. Each round-
topped petal has a double outline and a small dot
near its tip; at the juncture of petals are small palmettes. Bands of petals and relief squares decorate
the base and neck; the lid has triangles above and
below petals; on it a bull(?), with its legs folded, has
a traced collar and a broken rectangular lug behind
its neck (intact in 1954). Complete except for minor
chips. *Bronze.*

Height with lid 0.19 m　Diameter 0.058 m
Culican 1975, 111–2.
Acquired Spink & Son, 1957.

The long-necked flask without handles has a long
history in Western Asia. Examples of high status
materials begin with glass flasks in the mid-
second millennium BC. As Culican points out
however, the decoration of this flask has Achaemenid details even though exact parallels are
lacking. The minute palmettes between the tips
of the incised petals are placed in the same
manner as plainer ones on Xerxes' gold drinking
cup from Hamadan (Culican 1965, Pl 45). Such
subsidiary decoration was probably an abiding
legacy of Elamite tastes (*cf* Amiet 1966, Figs 261,

300, 375). Culican's argument, based on the
Pasyryk textiles, that it is an *ampulla* with a chain
originally securing the bull stopper to the vase,
carries less conviction since it is not certain that
the stopper belongs to the flask. The style of its
incised decoration and its material is different
from the body of the vessel. There is no corresponding lug for the chain on the flask itself, nor
are there wear marks around the knobbed base.
Its decoration militates against an Italic origin
and unless it proves to be a much later vessel, it
remains a unique Achaemenid work of severe
style, probably intended to contain unguents or
perfumes.

93

93　Spouted Bowl　28.43

Late 2nd–early 1st millennium BC.
Probably from North-West Iran.
Flat-based, deep bowl with rounded, incurving rim
and a wide, trough spout that tilts upwards. Wheel-
made, reddish-brown ware, stroke burnished.
Pottery.
Height 0.096 m　Diameter 0.184 (with spout)
Unpublished.
Acquired Winifred Williams, 1950.

This is almost identical with a spouted bowl
from the rich cemetery at Marlik in Gilan
(Negahban 1964, Fig 21) situated at the south-
west corner of the Caspian Sea. The archaeological record of this region is poorly known and the
date of some of the Marlik tombs is disputed.
Haerinck notes that this bowl type is very long-
lived but that by the eighth century BC most
examples are no longer burnished (1988, Figs
58.13, 14, 68.2, 3 and p 73).

92

III THE LEVANT

94–110

The Levant comprises the modern states of Cyprus, coastal Syria, Lebanon, Israel, Jordan and the southern part of Turkey known as Cilicia. This is topographically and environmentally a very mixed region of the Middle East. It includes arid zones flanking the Syrian desert in the east, fertile coastal margins facing the Mediterranean Sea in the west, swampland along the Orontes River in Syria and cedar clad mountains in Lebanon. This fragmented setting enjoined quite varied human responses so that urban dweller, farmer, pastoralist and nomad all co-existed here. Major factors which at one time or another distinguished the region are its small, competing city-kingdoms, its intermediate position between the great Assyro-Babylonian, Hittite and Egyptian Empires and its nuclear position as a crossroads for trade and contact between these Empires and between the whole regional network and Europe. Thus, in spite of the small scale of its constituent elements, peoples of the Levant played a pivotal role in many Near Eastern developments. They were responsible for such lasting achievements as simplified alphabetic scripts, unrivalled seafaring expertise and, in ancient times, two of the world's most influential religions, Judaism and Christianity.

Some of the earliest villages of the Near East are found in the Levant and it is here that man's transition through the various stages of foraging to sedentary farmer, one of the most profound changes in human evolution, may be closely and most rewardingly studied. The earliest sites with relatively permanent occupation occur inland where plentiful fauna such as gazelle were exploited so successfully. The Mediterranean littoral seems to have been avoided during this critical juncture, perhaps because too heavily forested. Already during the 8th and 7th millennia BC exchange in raw materials, a factor that subsequently characterised many economic systems of the area, plays an important part in developments.

During the 4th millennium BC there appeared along the bend of the Euphrates River in North Syria a number of precocious cities with monumental defences and public architecture. Tablets, seals and other evidence for complex society suggest that these may be intrusive early Sumerian merchant colonies. The effects of this enormous enterprise on local cultures, from whom the merchants presumably sought timber and other raw materials lacking to South Mesopotamia, are difficult to guage. When native urban centres emerge in the archaeological record of this region during the 3rd millennium BC, they immediately reveal an indebtedness, in the arts and writing for example, to ancient Sumer. A parallel case of long distance interaction occurred in the west at the foot of the Lebanon Mountains where the city of Byblos supplied timber and no doubt other goods to Egypt. Thereafter Byblos became the Asiatic city most profoundly influenced by Egyptian civilisation.

The immense inland Syrian city of Ebla with its remarkable archive written in Sumerian and West Semitic languages must have been a major focus of urban development. While cultural borrowing from Mesopotamia is evident, so too is a quite distinctive Syrian civilisation. To the south, in Palestine, heavily defended centres also appear in the settlement pattern of the third millennium BC, but there the absence of writing and other factors suggest that a different social system underlay the emergence of these secondary states. On the coast, the site of Byblos had already risen to pre-eminence in terms of imported metals and now Egyptian expeditions visited it in 'Byblos ships'. The third millennium therefore marks a fundamental turning point in the history of the Levant.

Most Palestinian urban centres were abandoned towards the end of the millennium. Other settlements suggest the development of a more rural settlement pattern, but destructions indicate that this rural movement was not altogether peaceful. Environmental deterioration, the retraction of Egyptian trade and Amorites, that is western Semitic peoples who are attested as marauders in Sumerian sources at this time, are some of the causative factors thought to be responsible for the transformation of urban-based society. Destruction levels are also evident in coastal cities of Anatolia and sites on Cyprus. It was therefore a period marked by more than one upheaval that may have affected several parts of the East Mediterranean basin.

In the ensuing Middle Bronze Age, kingdoms in the north, an area with signs of greater continuity, flourished in an international network of diplomatic, military and trade contacts. Texts from the royal archives at Mari reveal how Iamhad (Aleppo) was regarded as the strongest of several eminent city-states located in an enormous swathe of territory extending to Babylonia, how raw materials from the east were transported to coastal emporia like Ugarit in Syria for onward shipment across the Mediterranean to the west and how large groups of nomadic peoples interacted with these centralized authorities. Gifts and messengers from Middle Kingdom Egypt are attested particularly along the coastal fringes of the Levant. Somewhat before the downfall of Hammurabi's Dynasty in Babylon at the end of this period, the Hittites from Anatolia carried out successful campaigns in North Syria. Although theirs was an ephemeral conquest, it presaged events in the Late Bronze Age when the thriving Levantine city-states were parcelled out between contending Empires.

For much of the period *c* 1550–1200 BC the northern states were controlled by the Mitannians, a poorly understood confederacy of Indo-Europeans and Hurrians, and by the Hittites, while in the south the Canaanite city-states were absorbed into the Egyptian Empire of the New Kingdom. Letters from Amarna in Egypt and other texts show how many cities, particularly in the north, maintained a precarious independence or relative freedom under the constraints of vassal treaties. Society was dominated by palaces and wealth was increasingly concentrated there. Gift-giving at the highest levels, whether as tribute or to establish and maintain amicable relations between the Great Kings, who endearingly referred to themselves as 'brothers' in the royal correspondence of the day, reached unprecedented levels. To satisfy the demands for luxury products, master craftsmen and other specialists were exchanged between courts and truly international styles in the arts become evident.

Nowhere is this better seen than in the Levant. Craftsmen there had for long excelled in minor works of applied art, types more suitable for gift exchange than the grandiose architectural works of adjacent riverine civilisations. Thus, when Homer speaks of later Phoenician embossed and chased silverwork as 'surpassing by far all others on earth' he was in fact describing but the most recent proponents of a long established West Semitic, Levantine tradition.

In keeping with the character of Levantine production, this part of the collection has several small metal items and much of it belongs to the second millennium BC. Terracotta figurines (**94-5**) demonstrate Sumerian influence in cultic matters at the outset of this period, in the late 3rd–early 2nd millennia. A bull weight (**97**) is an expression of the importance of mercantile affairs, especially at coastal emporia. Perhaps the most significant object is the unique wooden head goblet (**100**) which so aptly conveys the eclectic refinements of the later Bronze Age. The disproportionately high number of objects from Cyprus is a consequence of the great interest of antiquarians in her prolific cemeteries and sanctuaries, coupled with ease of access and export in the later 19th and earlier 20th centuries. They include objects of the first millennium BC when decisive influence from the Greek mainland makes itself felt, as in the limestone head **110**.

There is only one possible object, a bronze cauldron protome (**105**), that may be attributed to the new states of the succeeding Iron Age on the Levantine mainland. The well known Phoenicians, Philistines and Israelites of that period are not represented in the collection

94 Head Of Figurine 28.84

Syrian (?) *c* 2500–2000 BC. Unprovenanced.

Part of stylised male figurine with chipped conical head, large broken ears, each pierced once, large eyes, each consisting of an applied ring and disc, aquiline nose with long, horizontally incised beard that conceals the mouth and chin. Cream-buff *terracotta*.

Height 0.044 m   Width 0.022 m
Unpublished.

95 Upper Part Of Figurine 28.83

Syrian (?) *c* 2500–1600 BC. Unprovenanced.

Head and upper torso of figurine with (missing) arms bent forward and traces of the hands on chest. Stylised head with large circular eyes in relief, nose and mouth chipped, pointed chin (beard?), traces of applied braid with incisions and flat hairlocks on cheeks. Impressed dots in a vertical row down the centre of the torso. Cream-buff *terracotta*.

Height 0.055 m   Width 0.041 m
Unpublished.

Terracotta figurines were mass produced in Bronze Age Mesopotamia and Syria and as the styles varied from area to area it is clear that there were numerous local workshops. While it is likely that many depicted divinities, the use and significance of most figurines is not well understood. Some may have been no more than toys. Better contextual information than is presently available will help in assessing their roles.

Heavily bearded figures like **94** are well known in third-second millennium BC Mesopotamia but they lack the enormous eyes and conical head of this example. Such features, together with pierced ears, are typical of terracottas from Syria (*cf* Badré 1980, Pls VI.120, XII.3, XXII.1). Given the absence of explicit divine attributes, it is likely to represent a human, but even this is not certain. The second figure is unusual in possessing what appears to be an unlikely row of buttons down its front. Its large eyes and distinctive hair braids occur on figurines in the area of the bend in the Euphrates River in northwest Syria (*cf* Badré 1980, Pls XLIII, XLIV.84), but its pointed chin is of a type more commonly found in coastal regions (*ibid* Pls LI.3–4, LVI.61).

94

95

96 Fenestrated Axehead 28.72

Syrian (?); Middle Bronze Age *c* 2000–
1700 BC. Unprovenanced.

Axehead, nearly semicircular in plan, the cutting
edge on the arc of the circle, the oval socket for the
shaft on its diameter. Two large, sub-circular fenestrations are placed side by side on the flat blade
and extend onto the socket to reveal the plain silver
sheet which encased the haft, originally of wood,
now missing. The maximum diameters of the oval
socket decrease from 0.026 m to 0.022 m, suggesting
a tapered handle. Corroded *bronze* blade, largely
intact and with a sharp cutting edge in places:
fragments of *silver* foil *in situ* in fenestration and
shaft hole. The silver was inserted as a grooved
sleeve, the groove opposite the blade intended to
secure the handle.

Height 0.125 m   Width 0.074 m

Sotheby 6.VII.1954, 22.151; Hannah 1956, 409.17;
Moorey & Schweizer 1972, 190.

Acquired G.F. Williams, 1954.

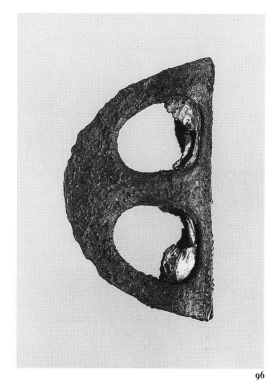

96

This highly specialized type of eye axe was particularly common in Syria during the Middle
Bronze I period. In keeping with the international character of that period however,
socketed eye axes had a much wider currency
and they are found in Iran in the east, the
merchant colony at Kultepe-Kanesh and other
sites in Anatolia in the north, on the island of
Cyprus in the west and on 12th Dynasty
paintings in Egypt in the south (Fig. 35).

The crescentic shape with eyes evolved from
two types: anchor axes, in which the sides of the
fenestrations did not join the socket, and others
with straight or curved cutting edges which were
secured to the handle by three rivetted tangs or
simply by curling the tips around the haft. While
many of these epsilon-shaped examples have
been found in Mesopotamia, they also occur in
Syria and hence the origin and evolution of the
type has a lengthy and complex history in which
the role of Syria should not be underestimated.
Another variant of the eye axe has an elongated,
duckbill shape. Often regarded as a later form of
the eye axe, its occurrence together with crescentic types like ours in the 'Tomb of the Lord of
the Goats' at Ebla (Weiss 1985, 243.117) and in
early contexts in Anatolia (Muscarella 1988b,
386–7) demonstrate that the two types co-existed
for some time.

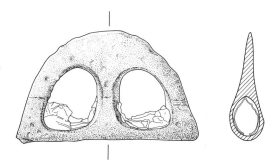

34   Fenestrated axehead 96.

35   Beni-hasan tomb painting with warriors carrying
weapons including a socketless version of 96 (*after*
Newberry 1923, Pl XVI).

The rich Ebla associations of the eye axe confirm the prestigious nature of this weapon. From its earliest appearance, as an epsilon type, it is depicted in the hands of gods and kings (Moortgat 1969, Pl N.2). Contemporary renderings, as on a basalt statue of a king from Ebla (Weiss 1985, 243) and on a seal from Tell el Dab'a in Egypt where it is held by a god identified as Baal (Porada 1984), confirm that its elite and ritual significance was still recognized. Indeed, the eyes of the crescentic type became so large that its effectiveness as a fighting weapon may be questioned. It is nonetheless shown in battle on an external panel of Thutmosis IV's chariot (Carter, Newberry 1904, Pls 10, 11). This scene is later (Thutmosis IV, c 1388–1379 BC) and the symbolism of such an archaic weapon may well have been devalued by that time. It is likely that during the Middle Bronze Age eye axes had both functional and ceremonial roles and that as they became more and more popular, their high status associations diminished. Moulds for their production were not uncommon and hence they were manufactured in several regions, and, at the outset at least, they presumably represented an internationally recognized system of status values.

One of the means whereby exclusively ceremonial axes may be distinguished from functional weapons is by material. Thus the fine gold examples from the Dépôt des Offrandes at Byblos are clearly ritual (Dunand 1950, Pls 133, 135). They are entirely of soft gold with the hafts between the eyes wrapped in gold foil which is sometimes decorated with geometric designs. The use of plain silver and tin bronze for the Burrell axe suggests a dual role.

Given the history of looting in the area of Byblos and the propensity for the use of precious metals in axes there, it would not be surprising if this example originally came from that coastal part of the Levant.

97 Bull Weight   28.30

Late Bronze Age c 1400–1200 BC. Unprovenanced, probably from the East Mediterranean basin area or Egypt.
Recumbent, hump-back bull facing left with slender body, tail swung up over haunches, large head modelled with horn stubs, protruding ears, swollen muzzle and no indication of eyes or mouth. Matchstick legs folded beneath body to form concave base now pierced with two screw-holes. The right hind leg is not indicated. Worn. *Leaded bronze.*
Present Weight (including the small stand screw and modern hole) 88.2 gr.
Height 0.034 m   Length 0.058 m   Thickness 0.02 m
Unpublished.
Acquired G.F. Williams, 1950.

Finely modelled reclining animals cast in bronze were used as weights especially during the 14–13th centuries BC in the East Mediterranean basin. Metalworkers cast quite a varied repertoire of species for this purpose: gazelle, pig, duck, frog, fish, felines and bovids (Yon 1987, 369). Of these, the bovids were most popular and they include cows, calves, sometimes with neck ring, and short-horned bulls. The reason for their popularity may have to do with a common perception that they are to be equated with wealth, just as in later times Latin *pecunia* (wealth) is derived from *pecus* (cattle) (Hayes 1959, 220).

These zoomorphs were normally hollow cast so that lead could be poured in to the required weight. This can be indicated by a series of strokes on the animals' backs, but the most satis-

factory way of ascribing a zoomorph to a weight system is by its actual weight. If allowance is made for weight depletion due to the modern screw holes in its base, then the Burrell weight represents 10 shekels of the Syrian system (1 shekel = 9.1/9.2 gr), the classic standard observed on many sites in the Levant (Courtois 1983, 126) and one that was also used in Egypt during the New Kingdom. During the Late Bronze Age there was a tendency for the shekel to decline in weight and this example may conform to such later values.

That the same animal type and weight standard is found so widely is due to the remarkable internationalism of the time. During the Late Bronze Age exchanges of gifts between great and small kings, all minutely accounted for, reached unprecedented heights. Such royal control of inter-regional trade is also echoed in later texts, the Elephantine papyri, in which weights are mentioned according to 'the stones of the king' (Stern 1982, 216). Examples of the latter, in stone or metal, are presumably depicted on 18th Dynasty tomb paintings where they are the property of the inspector of weights of precious metals. Fig. 36 shows how bull weights were placed on scale pans. Such pans are also frequently found in the Levant at this time (eg. Weiss 1985, 282.126). The royal connection is again evident on paintings of Hatschepsut's famed journey to the land of Punt. Balances with cow weights are there referred to as

> 'accurate and true, (balances) of Thoth which the King of Upper and Lower Egypt, Makere (Hatschepsut) made for her father, Amon, lord of Thebes, in order to weigh the silver, gold, lapis lazuli, malachite, and every splendid costly stone' (Breasted 1906, II.280).

When compared with the Mesopotamian stone duck weights (55–6) the values of the Levantine zoomorphs are quite small and hence they may have been reserved for precious commodities, as suggested by the Egyptian evidence.

Writing well before the discovery of many more examples from Cyprus, Catling speculated that weights from that island were brought home as curios (1964, 252 n.3). It now seems that the island was an integral part of this international system and one of the closest parallels for the

36 Zoomorphic weights used to weigh rings of precious metal. Egyptian painting of the New Kingdom (restored) (*after* Davies 1922, Pl 40).

Burrell weight is another reclining hump-backed bull with a total weight of 90.9 gr from the Cypriot city of Enkomi (Courtois 1984, 43.407, Pl III). A unique hoard of weights from the copper-mining centre of Kalavassos supplies further evidence for their concentration in Cyprus, their 14th–13th century *floruit* and their use. Here, in addition to the even more common ellipsoid haematite weights, was an impressive range of zoomorphs, including bovids, a negroid head weight and an exquisite cylinder seal (Courtois 1983, Pl 17). They were found in an administrative building and hence may have been used for the issue of purified copper. On the other hand, astonishing quantities of gold were found in a somewhat earlier tomb at this city and so the weights may have been used for dispensing gold to craftsmen to fashion particular pieces of jewellery.

Most examples come from the Levantine mainland (eg Anderson 1988, Pl 39.12) where this metal type was clearly at home, but the international character of zoomorphic weights at this time means that it is not possible to specify an origin for the Burrell weight more closely than the East Mediterranean basin, including Egypt. Even such an ascription may be overly specific since it is now clear from a contemporary shipwreck off the Turkish coast at Ulu Burun (Kaş) that such weights were carried by merchants or messengers on precocious transmaritime ventures (Pulak 1988, 30, Fig 37 bottom right). The main cargo of this ship was copper ingots of a distinctive oxhide shape which have been found as far away as the Black Sea and Sardinia. Indeed, the inclusion of a bovid weight on the Ulu Burun ship points to the likelihood that a passenger, if not the owner himself, operated an accounting system typical of the Levant.

One unusual feature distinguishes this weight. While most were apparently hollow cast for the insertion of lead to the correct weight, it consists of bronze alloyed with lead (Appendix A). Typical weights retain clear traces of the outline of the hollow for the lead on their bases. Courtois knows of no others made of leaded bronze, but, as he points out, few analyses have been undertaken (pers comm 14.III.89) and so it is not possible to state how exceptional this more sophisticated example is at present.

98   Bull Figurine   28.42

Bronze Age *c* 3000–1000 BC. Unprovenanced, possibly Syrian.

Standing, partly sheathed hump-backed bull with narrow body and haunches, straight tail, large shoulders and relatively massive head with protruding short horns curled forward. Relief ridge along chest and trace of a strap (?), width 0.006 m, around the midriff immediately behind the small hump. Modelled details obscured by the corrosion with dark, red-brown patina. Legs missing, modern dowel holes.

Bronze with silver plating.

Height 0.052 m   Length 0.064 m Thickness 0.03 m
Hannah 1953, 112.1.

Acquired Winifred Williams, 1950.

99   Bull Figurine   28.31

Late Bronze Age *c* 1550–1050 BC. Unprovenanced, probably from Cyprus or Syria.

Standing, hump-backed bull with long body, its head slightly raised. Deep, hanging dewlap, short horns upright above ears, protruding at right angles to head; dot-and-circle eyes lightly modelled, sensitive muzzle. Corrosion obscures detail: there is a lack of incision work and modelling is bold; socket (?) for missing right hind leg. *Bronze* with brown and red patina, swollen surface texture.

Height 0.053 m   Length 0.092 m Thickness 0.03 m
McLellan Galleries 6 illus; Exh. Glasgow 1949, no. 138.

Acquired John Hunt, 1948.

The powerful symbolism of bulls was not lost on ancient Near Eastern cultures and so the bull frequently occurs as single figures or in elaborate compositions (*cf* **15–18**). This ubiquity, the absence of a general iconographical study of bull representations and the poor state of preservation of these two examples make their ascription to metalworkers of a particular culture zone a speculative exercise.

Standing animals executed in metal first occur in South Mesopotamia in the Protoliterate Period (Heinrich 1936, Pl 13a, lion amulet). At that time the lower legs of animals were sometimes made of different materials and this could explain the socket of the hind leg of **99**. The midriff strap of **98** also finds a parallel of that time on the silver zoomorph crowning a lapis lazuli seal from *Sammelfunde* Pa XVI₂ at Uruk (Behm Blancke 1979, Pl 8.45). Yet, metal figurines then are rare, animal figurines are

normally shown with their heads *en face*, and the socket is so ill-formed it may simply be a break that reveals a casting hollow.

Several features of **99** rather suggest a Cypriot or Syrian source of the Late Bronze Age. Its hump, elongated body and dot-and-circle eyes are characteristic features of bull figures from the island of Cyprus (Catling 1964, Pls 43 b, d, g, h, 44a, b; Courtois 1984, Pl. IV.2). The last feature is also typical of contemporary Cypriot clay bulls (e.g. Weiss 1985, 290, 314.139) as well as anthropomorphic figurines (Courtois 1984, Pls VII, IX). During this period, Cyprus shared many artistic trends and political fortunes with Syria and hence it is not surprising to find parallels there too, though they are not so common (Hrouda 1962, Pl. 2.15).

Bulls are pre-eminent in Cypriot cults from the time the species was introduced to the island at the beginning of the Bronze Age. Large portions of the animals were interred with the dead then and in the Late Bronze Age these were replaced by small bull statuettes. The latter have also been found in sanctuaries as foundation deposits, or more likely, as votives. In the absence of textual evidence and explicit iconographical details the exact role(s) of bull figurines in Cypriot religion is uncertain (Loulloupis 1979).

The strap on **98** may eventually help to elucidate its cultural context. An example of similar style with gold inlay apparently comes from North Syria (Ash Mus 1955.42). Bronze or copper animal figurines partly sheathed in silver may have been widespread. They are particularly distinctive of Early Bronze Age Anatolia (*cf PK* 14, Pl XL) where, according to Mesopotamian tradition, the Silver Mountain was located.

The appreciable inclusion of iron in **99** could conceivably be the result of the use of iron-rich sulphide ores (see also Appendix A). Fluxes however were not always successful in removing iron in the smelting process. As iron is typical of Near Eastern smelting processes in general, its inclusion at high levels in **99** cannot indicate the source of the object or the ore from which it was made.

100 Head Goblet 13.230

Levantine; Late Bronze Age *c* 1400–1200 BC. Allegedly found in Egypt in a tomb of the XIIth Dynasty.

Small, incomplete goblet, its cup carved in the shape of a female head, its base designed as her neck decorated with three rows of incised triangles and alternating squares and rectangles, probably representing a multiple stranded necklace. Sensitively modelled face with narrow, pointed chin, inlaid eyes (right one missing), separate eye brows in low relief and hair indicated by a relief band with obliquely combed incisions over the forehead and across the remaining ear, with a thicker plait wound round the head above this fringe. The ear, which protrudes through and below the hair, carries a drop-shaped earring and, in front of it, on her cheek, is a poorly cut incision or a chip. A plain band (traces of

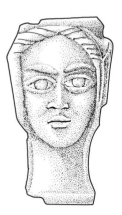

incised triangles?) is placed between the hair and rim, and a single, vertical lug hole remains on the unpolished interior. Back of head and right side of face missing. Carved from a single block of *prunus* or *crategus wood* with inlaid eyes of fibrous wood (?) and harder wood or mineral (?) pupil. See Appendix A.

Height 0.107 m   Width 0.048 m

Culican 1961, 141, Fig 15; 1971, Pls XXVII–XXVIII; Peltenburg 1972, 134–5, Pl XXIV.1.

Acquired G.F. Williams, 1953.

The wood from which this goblet was carved, blackthorn or boxwood, inhabits areas outside Egypt according to Culican (1971, 86 n.1). These species are known in such East Mediterranean lands as Cyprus and Lebanon. As both regions shipped timber to Egypt during the Late Bronze Age, a period when there are close analogies for the head goblet, the wood cannot fix its origins securely. These analogies however are all well known Asiatic types without Egyptian parallels and so, if it was found in Egypt, the presumption must be that it was imported as a finished product or made there under Asiatic influence.

The analogies just mentioned were made of polychrome glazed faience at a number of Western Asiatic centres (Figs 38–40). They are confined to the late 14th–13th centuries BC and while relatively common in North Syria and Cyprus, their distribution is remarkably extensive (Frankfort 1970, 274–6; Weiss 1985, 294.146). Their narrow date range precludes the ascription of the Burrell goblet by antiquity market sources to a Middle Kingdom tomb of the 12th Dynasty (unless the tomb was re-used later). So similar are these colourful faiences that our example may also have been gaudily painted or overlaid at one time, but of this nothing survives save the slightly discoloured eyes. They sometimes occur in temples dedicated to local versions of the goddess Ishtar, but to refer to them as 'Ishtar cups' suggests that they represent that goddess and there is still too little evidence for such an identification.

While the similarities to the faience versions are undoubtedly close enough to warrant a similar date for the wooden goblet, there are fine but significant stylistic differences which reveal that the carver worked in another, kindred tradition. This is most clearly evident in the eyes which are almond shaped rather than the frequently large ovals or circles of the faiences.

39 Faience head goblet fragment from Tell Abu Hawam
    (*after* Hamilton 1935, 65, Pl 28.425)

40 Faience head goblet from Ashur (*after* Andrae 1935,
    79, Fig 62).

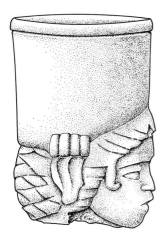

These almond shapes are clearly an Egyptianising trait that lends to the face an entirely distinct aspect, one which lacks the fixed, at times incredulous, stare of the faiences. Faces of the latter are often highlighted by haircurls applied to the forehead and cheeks (Fig 39), but the wood carver has deliberately excluded such an exotic coiffure (unless the cheek mark originally secured an appliqué). There are further, minor, differences. With a height of just over 10 cms it is rather smaller than the faiences (heights in the Levant are about 15 cms), there is possible additional decoration below the rim, hair is more finely rendered, earring is unique, the side and probably the back of the neck are left exposed and the base is poorly articulated. Culican (1971) suggested that the holes in the nose were to hold a nose-ring as on certain Palestinian faience head goblets, but there are no holes, only a shallow transverse groove on the underside of the nose. This indentation is simply a stylistic feature and it could not have retained a nose ring.

While stylistic variation is also evident amongst the faiences, none has the sensitive modelling and Egyptian treatment of the eyes as here. There is no reason why faience-workers could not have achieved similar results and hence this carver was not just working in a different

medium but rather in another milieu and perhaps for a distinct clientele. Since wood rarely survives in Levantine soil conditions and the wood of the goblet is in such good condition, it probably does come from Egypt where it was sent some time during the late 18th–20th Dynasties. That head goblets were transported and not just made by craftsmen attached to temples or palaces for local distribution is confirmed by the presence of faience ones on the Ulu Burun (Kaş) shipwreck off the South Anatolian coast (Pulak 1988, 32, Fig 40). Why it was sent and how it was perceived in Egypt is another matter, though it should be noted that a large Asiatic population dwelt there at this time. The sacred and funerary contexts of its faience parallels indicate that head goblets exemplify a high status ideology in society and that they should not be considered merely as traded bric-à-brac. The amalgamation of Egyptian stylistic traits and an Asiatic concept is typical of Egyptianising ateliers in the Levant.

The Burrell head goblet is thus a significant addition to the known corpus of such remarkable objects. For the first time it demonstrates the existence of an Egyptianising style within this class, production in wood and not just faience which survives better in Asiatic soil conditions and a notable extension to their distribution.

101 Red Polished Jug 19.91

Middle Cypriot Bronze Age *c* 1900–1800
BC. Unprovenanced, probably from
Cyprus.

Globular jug with slightly flattened base, tall narrow
neck with everted rim and single twisted handle
from shoulder to mid-neck. Two small knobs and,
opposite the handle, one disc on shoulder. On the
last is a syllabic symbol with three more lines below
it and other signs arranged to left, right and below,
all incised after firing and encrusted with a white
paste. *Pottery* with all over burnish, differentially
blackened by reduction.

Height 0.447 m Diameter 0.33 m

Unpublished.

Acquired W. Williams, 1949.

During the Early and Middle Bronze Ages
in Cyprus, *c* 2300–1600 BC, chamber tombs
located in extensive cemeteries were often
lavishly equipped with large numbers of Red
Polished pots. The fact that this example is intact

strongly suggests that it comes from one such
tomb, perhaps in the north or eastern part of the
island. Its shape is fairly late in the typological
development of this long-lived ware, but because
of disturbances in tombs, there are few dating
controls.

Two special features on the jug call for
comment. Its twisted vertical handle is unusual
since most handles are plain or bear crossed
incised decoration. The latter may be a simplified version of this modelled rendering which in
turn could have copied twisted rope used to carry
gourds, the natural shape which served as models
for pottery jugs of this type. Another jug with
twisted handle and more elaborate shoulder
decoration is in Edinburgh (Goring 1988, 45.40).
Twisted handles more commonly occur on
smaller jugs with cut-away spouts, like one from
the rich cemetery at Lapithos (*SCE* IV.IA, Fig.
LXV. 5, 6).

The incised signs (Fig 41) belong to the Cy-
pro-Syllabic script which was developed on the
island some thousand years later. It has fifty to
sixty signs, is read from right to left and was used
to write Greek and the native, undeciphered
Eteo-Cypriot. It became common in the 6th
century and ceased to be used *c* 200 BC. While
it was occasionally written on pottery, and
sometimes earlier pots were re-used and inscribed, it is quite extraordinary to find this
script on Red Polished pottery. O. Masson refers
to other Cypriot vessels similarly inscribed with
deep, post-firing, white-filled incisions that he
believes to be falsifications of the late 19th
century AD (pers comm). The inscription
therefore is likely to be a modern addition (*cf.*
CVA Louvre 5, 1982, 33).

41 Inscription on **101**.

102 Black Slip Juglet 19.70

Middle Cypriot III–Late Cypriot I
period, *c* 1725–1450 BC. Unprovenanced,
probably from Cyprus.

Juglet with slight hollow base, ovoid body, narrow
neck, everted rim and strap handle from shoulder to
mid-neck. Finely incised decoration consists of three
vertical bands filled with plain lozenges with
hatched borders alternating with zigzag-filled bands
and a cross-hatched band that extends onto the
handle. Hatched triangles on the shoulder and a
band of plain lozenges with hatched borders at mid-
neck. *Pottery* with worn, burnished surface.

Height 0.228   Diameter 0.155 m

Unpublished.

Acquired W. Williams, 1948.

During the first half of the second millennium
BC in the Eastern Mediterranean basin there
appeared an exceptionally varied series of juglets
with narrow necks. They were traded in large
numbers and it is often assumed that the decoration on the juglets served as a hallmark of the
type of scented perfume, opium or other substances which they contained. The Egyptians
were particularly zealous in obtaining specialty
oils for rituals and other purposes, and foreign
juglets are found there in large numbers. This
example belongs to a period when Cypriot
juglets were beginning to appear in foreign
markets in increasing numbers. The type
normally has more coarsely incised decoration
and a small disc base. The shape is in fact more
common in other Cypriot wares such as early
Base Ring and Red-on-Black ware juglets, hence
it should belong to the mid-second millennium
BC. It must have come from an atelier that
excelled in quality products, perhaps to be
located in the east (*cf* Frankel 1983, Pl 29.883) or
near the Bay of Morphou in the northwest of the
island.

103 White Slip II Tankard 19.43

Late Cypriot Bronze Age *c* 1400–1200
BC. Unprovenanced, probably from
Cyprus.

Ring-based tankard with globular body, wide neck,
everted ledge rim, strap handle from shoulder to
rim where there is a chipped tab which probably
once had projections like those on the shoulder tab
opposite. Body decorated with vertical framed rows
of hatched lozenges alternating with ladders, all
pendant from a horizontal ladder on the shoulder.
On the neck, two horizontal rows of four lines interrupted by framed double rows of hatched lozenges.

Groups of four strokes on the rim, wavy line borders below on the handle, tab projection and has a cross on the base. *Pottery* with brown paint on grey/buff slip; red/brown grit-tempered clay.

Unpublished. Exh. Glasgow 1949, No. 94.

Height 0.203, Width 0.139 m

Acquired W. Williams, 1948.

This type of painted pottery is one of the most distinctive hallmarks of prehistoric Cypriot ceramic production. Produced by hand rather than on the wheel as was normal for pottery in adjacent lands at the time, this White Slip pottery, as it is known, nonetheless enjoyed tremendous popularity both at home and abroad in Egypt and the Levantine mainland during the most prosperous phase of the island's early history. Bowls were more commonly exported and although they often served as lids for jars abroad, they must have been prized primarily for their aesthetic appeal rather than any contents or secondary function. While it is possible that this tankard could have been found outside Cyprus, it is much more likely to have come from the island itself.

Its rather slipshod painted decoration places it in the middle range of the evolution of White Slip pottery. Provenanced examples from Cyprus come mainly from the southeast where there are many examples with identical patterns and shoulder tabs (*SCE* IV. 1C, 448–9, Figs 52 top left, 53.9 type 1a). The handle tab was presumably meant to lever open a hinged lid on wood or metal tankards, but it has become an essentially decorative thumb grip on this pottery copy.

104 Bichrome II–III Amphora 19.26

Cypro-Geometric II–III period, *c* 950–750 BC. Unprovenanced, probably from Cyprus.

Amphora with ovoid body, straight, wide neck, flat everted rim, two opposed horizontal shoulder handles and ring base. Decoration in matt black paint except for a central red neck band on plain buff surface. Strokes on rim, groups of thick and thin bands on neck and body, single wavy band between solidly painted handles. *Pottery.*

Height 0.34 m Diameter 0.228 m

Unpublished.

Acquired W. Williams, 1948.

During the Iron Age in Cyprus potters developed a series of very well defined pottery types based on forms that emerged at the transition with the preceding Late Bronze Age. The spare, neatly executed decoration of this amphora also recalls compositions that are first seen after the destruction of the Mycenaean palaces in Greece and hence the origins of the type has its roots in the great upheavals *c* 1200 BC which brought Cyprus into ever closer contact with Greece. The intact state of this amphora indicates that it comes from a tomb. These were placed in cemeteries and comprise types ranging from simple chambers to built chambers approached by a wide avenue or *dromos*. Amphorae were commonly interred with the dead and on one famous example, the Hubbard Amphora, a feasting scene provides explicit information on the use of these vessels in rituals (Gjerstad 1960, Fig 14.4). Amphorae from the 'royal' necropolis at Salamis were used for a variety of purposes, some as receptacles for the incinerated bones of the dead, others for olive oil, as an inscription on one informs us (Karageorghis 1969, Pls 24, 28).

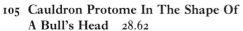

105 Cauldron Protome In The Shape Of A Bull's Head   28.62

Syrian (?) late 8th–7th centuries BC. Unprovenanced.

Hollow, cast bull's head with flat, triangular flange, now worn, extending around its base and a loop on its back. The head is wide and short, only the stubs of the forward curving horns remain, the muzzle is poorly articulated and there are slight remains of traced decoration. Eyes consist of two or three concentric circles, and from them pairs of lines loop around the base of the horns (visible clearly in one case only). There are similar bands from the ears to the muzzle which is outlined by one or two hatched bands. A single traced line extends through the broken mouth. Incomplete; remains of one rivet in the attachment flange. Cast and traced *bronze*.

Height 0.078;   Width 0.073;   Depth 0.045 m.

Unpublished.

Acquired W. Williams, 1948.

The worn, flanged base of this bull's head, with traces of a rivet, indicate that it was once attached to another object. The loop on its back would have secured a ring for a handle. These features and the few stylistic elements still visible on the much damaged head identify its original use as a cauldron protome.

While functionally the same as such metropolitan Urartian protomes as **60**, there are a number of stylistic features that distinguish it.

The head is cast together with the attachment plaque, it possesses a ring for a handle, ears are bent forward, horns are shorter and details such as eyes and 'collar' are much simplified. Decoration, furthermore, is largely traced rather than executed in plastic form. These aspects of the head link it to another well-known group of broadly contemporary cauldron protomes from Mediterranean lands (*cf* Amandry 1956, 245; Jantzen 1972, 78–9, Pls 76–7). In Italy and Greece such prestige goods belong to an orientalising phase when eastern products became highly fashionable, and with them eastern cultural influence to be emulated, adapted or rejected according to circumstances.

A small intact cauldron with bull handle mounts, allegedly from Cumae in Italy, shows how this head was originally placed with one or more other protomes below the rim (Fig 43). They are attached to the body of the cauldron by birds' wings whereas this example has no more than a triangular base plate by which it was fixed directly to the vessel. In spite of this difference, the Burrell head closely resembles that from Cumae in terms of its compact plump form, short horns bent forward and extensive use of traced details such as the strokes between the eyes. In his study of cauldron attachments from Olympia, Herrmann identified certain protomes from Gordion, Samos, Delphi and Olympia that also shared many features with the Cumae

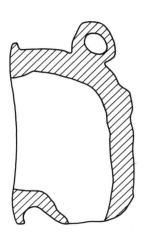
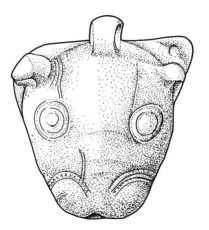
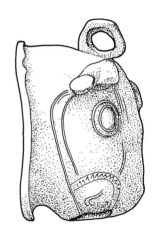

protomes and he assembled these in a stylistically homogeneous 'Cumae-Group', to be dated to the late 8th–7th centuries BC (1966, 123–130). It is characterised by a single piece construction, compact, rounded heads, short horns curving inward over the head and triangular attachment plates. Within this group only the Burrell, Gordion (Tumulus W) and Cumae heads have handle rings and extensive linear patterns worked into the surface; the Cumae and Burrell heads also have rather unnaturalistic circular eyes. It shares with the Gordion cast heads and other members of the group the same distinctive triangular attachment plate. In spite of its poor state of preservation therefore, the Burrell protome may be attributed to this group.

While other scholars regard the Cumae head as Phrygian, Herrmann persuasively proposed a North Syrian derivation (1966, 128) and this has met with increasing acceptance. Certainly the recently discovered Phrygian cauldron from Tumulus D at Bayınder Elmalı, which was associated with a Phrygian inscribed silver ladle, carries more simplified bulls' head protomes than the Burrell head (Özgen & Özgen 1988, 35.33).

Muscarella has detailed many of the characteristics of several manufacturing centres (1988b, 263 n.1). The difficulty with the proposal of a North Syrian centre has always been the dearth of cauldron protomes from that region, but such a paucity is most likely due to lack of excavations, especially when compared with the relative concentration of more recent work in the west. That North Syrian bronzeworkers were already

42 Cauldron protome **105**.

43 Cauldron allegedly from Cumae (*after* Amandry 1956, Pl 28).

familiar with zoomorphic attachments to vessels at least by the Late Bronze Age is evident from a vessel with such animal embellishments from Meskene-Emar (see **60**). More Iron Age examples from North Syria are required to provide a clear idea of the range of protome production in an area of competing kingdoms which, according to Assyrian sources, were rich in metalwork.

Due to the widespread distribution of this type of bull protome, it is not possible to fix its provenance more precisely than the Levant, Western Anatolia or the East and Central Mediterranean regions. Since it is of cast rather than beaten metal it is more likely to have been made in the east. The rivet has much less tin than the head itself (Appendix A) and this intentional difference was to make it more malleable for fastening purposes.

c 700–475 B C. Unprovenanced, East
Mediterranean.

Slender-bodied horse with long straight legs,
upright neck, small head, ears pricked forward
beside forelock and raised, flat tail. Coarsely
modelled rider perches without a saddle on its back
and holds right arm aloft and a circular shield with
large flat boss in his left. Surfaces eroded but traces
of paint on horse's legs, mane and neck, and on
rider's right arm, torso, neck and shield. *Terracotta*
with yellowish, grit-tempered surface.
Height 0.142 m   Length 0.145 m
Unpublished.
Acquired Spink & Son, 1954.

Small terracotta models of warriors on horseback
were extremely popular in the middle of the first
millennium B C in East Mediterranean regions,
nowhere more so than in Cyprus. At that time
the island was divided into ten or twelve vying
kingdoms. As the cemeteries at Salamis indicate,
the rich, perhaps only the royal family, had horse
drawn vehicles, while many of the lower classes
in the Cellarka cemetery were cavalrymen if one
may judge from the number of mounted warrior
figurines recovered from graves (Karageorghis
1969). These burials and representations on
pottery show that considerable expenditure was
lavished on the display of personal and equestrian paraphernalia. The precise role and
number of horsemen in Cypriot Iron Age
society, for both fighting and ceremonial
purposes, is unknown. A second major source of

horsemen figurines is from votive deposits in
shrines and temples, particularly from the
temple dedicated to Apollo at Kourion.

The Cypriot origin of this figurine is by no
means certain. Regional styles existed and these
are typically simple without pretence to realism
(*cf SCE* II, Pl 234.1). Unlike this rendering,
most examples consist of horseriders seated close
to the mane which they grasp with both hands.
The short head and long thin legs and tail of this
horse are also unusual in Cyprus. That the rider
is apparently seated in a slight depression in,
rather than on the horse's back also raises
questions about the integrity of the piece.

Schematized horseriders wielding a spear and
shield as here (the spear is lost) are widespread in
the East Mediterranean and there are also close
parallels from Rhodes and western Asia Minor
(*cf* Higgins 1954, Pl 51.301), some imported
from Cyprus.

107 Female Figure 19.135

Cypro-Archaic II period *c* 600–475 B C.
Unprovenanced, probably from Cyprus.

Female standing with right arm in front, the hand
clasping a bird, left arm along side holding an un-
identified object. Face with almond-shaped eyes,
plain triangular nose, small mouth and protruding
chin. She wears a peaked cap or *polos*, its front decorated with strokes and stabs, a long tunic with no
details save for the ends of a sash depending in
front of the simply bordered hem immediately above
exposed feet. The hair extends in plaits to her
shoulders and elaborate jewellery consists of drop-
shaped earrings, choker with central clasp and
pendants, two-stranded necklace of biconical beads
and central pendants above a bar-shaped pendant;
armlets on her left arm. Hollow, mould-made *terracotta*, with traces of red paint on and above breasts,
blackened hair, hollow body with vent holes in head
and back.
Height 0.36 m   Width 0.11 m
Unpublished.
Acquired Spink & Son, 1955.

Astonishing numbers of votive figurines were
placed in the many rural shrines and urban sanctuaries of Iron Age Cyprus. One of the most

common type is the richly caparisoned female bearing a gift. Their highly standardized but elaborate jewellery probably reflects that which adorned the cult statue or it may symbolize the status of the devotee. These females are likely to have been priestesses or members of the upper classes. Save for those with uplifted arms and tall hats, the figurines are unlikely to represent goddesses, but their occurrence in large numbers in sanctuaries very likely indicates the presence of a female cult.

As in the case of all terracotta production, there are regional styles. In general terms this figure belongs to Gjerstad's Neo-Cypriot style of terracotta sculptures (cf SCE IV.2, 105–7). This style flourished in the eastern part of the island and some of the closest analogies come from the *temenos* of a temple at Arsos which was excavated in 1917 by Markides and subsequently published by the Swedes (SCE III, 583). Figurines from it

are shown in a number of postures, the most elaborate clasping an object in their right hand which is crossed before the body as here. In common with many Cypriot shrines where there is marked continuity of worship through major political and social changes, the Arsos shrine functioned for a long time, from the Late Bronze Age to Early Christian period.

Almost identical figurines were installed in sanctuaries on the islands of Rhodes and Samos to the west. Such was their impact that western coroplasts often imitated these Cypriot figurines.

108 Horse's Head   28.86

First millennium BC. Unprovenanced.
Worn head perforated from mouth to interior and broken from larger figure. Plain, with circular sockets for lost eye pellets, broken ears and arched mane, traces of headstall crossed between eyes and extending to either side of the mouth. Brown-buff hollow *terracotta* with pinkish surface.
Length 0.055 m   Height 0.05 m
Unpublished.

While simplified models of horses begin in the early second millennium BC in the Near East, their *floruit* occurs much later, during the Achaemenid Period when horse and rider figures became extremely popular. In Cyprus, horses were also frequently sculpted by themselves or as part of a chariot group, but a crossed bridle would be unusual on the island. The pinkish surface, cross strap and large eyes of this example recall Achaemenid examples (cf Stern 1982, 167, Fig 286).

109 Male Head 28.85

First millennium BC. Unprovenanced.

Male head broken from larger figure. High, pointed headgear with broken forward projection, horizontal relief band on forehead, visible only as discoloured impression on side of head, socketed eyes, one retaining a circular pellet, mouth indicated by skewed scratch and short, squared beard or chin. Pinkish-buff *terracotta*, chipped and worn.

Height 0.057 m   Width 0.025 m

Unpublished.

The distinctive headdress of this head, although broken, resembles the 'Phrygian cap', a misnomer for high tiaras with rolled base that became popular during the Achaemenid Period. These figures are widespread in the Near East, though pellet eyes would be unusual in Cyprus.

110 Head Of Worshipper 19.152

Cypro-Archaic II–Cypro Classical I *c* 600–400 BC. Unprovenanced, probably from Cyprus.

Male head broken at base of neck. Beardless face with faint smile, oval eyes set asymmetrically, hair over the top of the head rendered by parallel grooves and a double fringe below a wreath of myrtle and berries. Restored nose. *Limestone*.

Height 0.165 m   Width 0.113 m

Unpublished.

Acquired Spink & Son, 1954.

During the later 7th and 6th centuries BC Cypriot coroplasts and sculptors began to adopt some of the developments towards naturalism in representative art that were being made in the Greek world. The taut, severe abstractions of native Cypriot expressions yielded to this new influence in many regions of the island and our head exemplifies that process. Its softer, beardless features, smile and hair wreath or fillet are radical departures from established traditions.

The head belongs to the Archaic Cypro-Greek style known from the many temples and shrines of Iron Age Cyprus (*cf SCE* III, Pl 115). The full figure, meant to stand as a substitute for the votary in a temple, would have had one leg slightly in front of the other, been dressed with a linen tunic (*chiton*) and woollen cloak (*himation*) and would have held an offering or had its arms raised in a gesture of adoration.

IV MISCELLANEOUS QUERIES PASTICHES AND FAKES

Certain artefacts in the Collection were acquired as Western Asiatic antiquities, but in some cases it is possible to demonstrate that they are probably fakes and in other cases the attribution is suspect or problematic. These objects are briefly listed here as a contribution to a better understanding of modern tastes and the recent history of the art and antiquities market. The problem of fakes is a widespread one and examples are included in an effort to undermine the illegal business of forgery and to promote the practice of legitimate acquisition from scientifically controlled excavations. Also in the following inventory are objects that may well be genuine. Sir William left no information regarding their alleged provenances and their attribution to specific cultures or periods on stylistic grounds has proved difficult. Scholars are invited to supply further information.

111 Spouted Vessel 28.79

Unprovenanced, possibly from West Iran or Mesopotamia.

Plain, flat based bowl with slightly convex, vertical wall, thickened rim and deep, narrow spout tilted upwards. *Silver*. Slightly distorted by compression along the axis of the spout, causing rim cracks. Repaired base.

Height 0.158 m   Diameter 0.221 × 0.117 m

Wells 1960, 189.5.

Acquired Spink & Son, 1956.

Metal bowls with such distinctive long spouts as this occur principally during two periods in the ancient Near East: during the second half of the third millennium in Luristan, Elam (LeBreton 1957, 109, Fig 27.3, of lead) and Sumer, and in the first millennium BC. The former group (*cf* Nagel 1963, Pl LXXV. 1–6) provides the closest, though not precise analogies; their spouts are finer and they are all of bronze or copper (Amiet 1986, Fig. 161).

The anomalously high proportion of zinc in this vessel casts doubt on its antiquity (see Appendix A).

112 Armlet 33.191

Unprovenanced.

Penannular armlet with animal head terminals. They have snub noses and circular bosses for eyes to which the long relief ears are connected. Manes are indicated by a groove with traced herring-bone design on either side. Three sets of engraved rings near terminals. *Brass*.

Diameter 0.129 m × 0.11 m

Unpublished.

Acquired A. Garabed, 1953.

The high zinc content of the terminals and bar indicate that this is a recent attempt to copy Luristan bracelets somewhat like **77** (see Appendix A). It is however larger than **77** and more specific models are extant armlets of the type worn on the upper arms of figures in Neo-Assyrian relief sculptures of the 9th–7th centuries BC (*cf* Hrouda 1965, Pls 9.9–12, 34.2, 36.1,3 *passim*).

113 Anthropomorphic Jug 19.110

Unprovenanced.

Jug with ovoid body, slightly pointed base and banded neck terminating in grotesque head. The male head has a disc-shaped cap, deeply socketed eyes, incised lines and gaping mouth. Broken arms and penis, navel protuberance and short spout in chest. Burnished red *pottery*.

Height 0.47 m.   Diameter 0.21 m

Unpublished.

Acquired W. Williams, 1949.

Although the imaginative Cypriot potters exuberantly transformed mouths of jugs into human heads from the Chalcolithic period onwards (*cf SCE* IV.2. Fig 29.20 *passim*), and execution becomes more varied and slovenly during the Cypro-Classical Period, there are no good Cypriot parallels for this jug. Possibly from Ibiza (*cf. i Fenici*, 345 left).

114 Group Of Three Hippopotami 28.9

Unprovenanced.

Three adjacent and parallel hippopotami are roughly chiselled from a single block of *limestone*. The lower bodies merge with the base, as if this composite is incompletely finished.

Length 0.062 m   Depth 0.055 m

Exh. Glasgow 1949, No. 117; *McLellan Galleries* 9, right ill.

Acquired Spink & Son, 1948.

While small representations of hippopotami occur frequently in Egypt and they are also known at Byblos in the Levant, such objects are usually made of faience as single figures and not as triads. There are no Sumerian examples (*contra McLellan Galleries* 9, right).

115 Bracelet 28.13

Unprovenanced.

Heavy *variegated stone* annular ring, polished, with plano-convex section.

Diameter 0.095 m

Unpublished. Exh. Glasgow 1949, No. 149.

Acquired John Hunt, 1948.

Similarly shaped armlets and bracelets occur in Egypt especially during the 1st–3rd Dynasties, but they are not known to have been exported to Western Asia. Shell, ivory and bone were the favoured materials. Armlets made of stone are usually of alabaster.

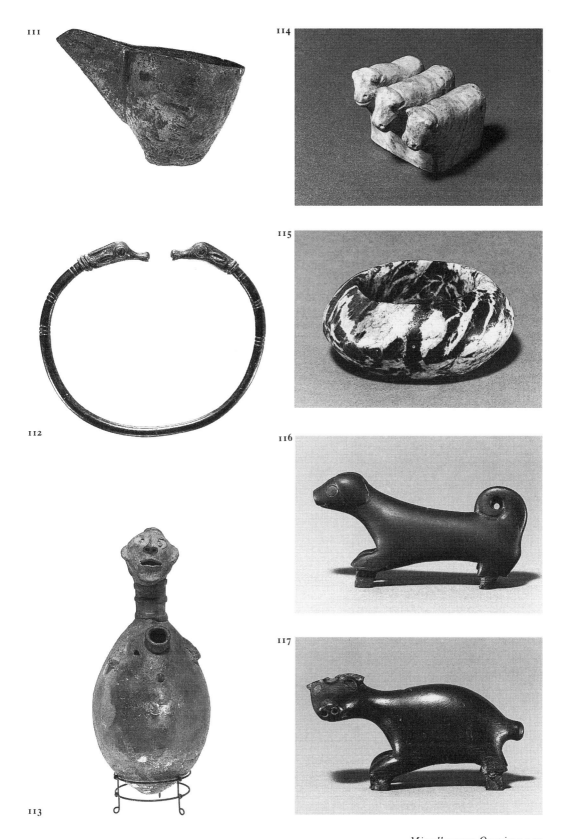

111

114

112

115

116

113

117

116–7 Dog Figures 28.27–8

Unprovenanced.

Two dog-like figures, both with large floppy ears,
inlaid eyes and paws with projecting tenons. One with
thick curled tail, the other, *regardant*, with short
stubby tail. Dark black, polished *stone* with inlaid eyes
of reddish-black schist.
Lengths 0.092 m.
Exh. Glasgow 1949, Nos. 134, 135; *McLellan Galleries*
6, bottom ill.
Acquired John Hunt, 1948.

Representations of dogs in Mesopotamia first
appear in terracotta as votives in the Old Babylonian period when they are associated with the
cult of Gula. In Neo-Assyrian times figures of
dogs in metal and terracotta were buried under
temples and shrines to deter evil. Both the
material and the style of these are unusual in
pre-Hellenistic contexts (but *cf* bronze
'panthers' of the Parthian (?) period: *Sotheby's*
7.11.1977, No. 47). They are unlikely to be
Sumerian as stated in *McLellan Galleries* 6,
bottom.

118 Smiting God Figure 28.32

Unprovenanced.

Striding male figure with right arm raised, left
extended. Concave-sided tall headdress with low
relief horns, socketed eyes, smoothly bearded face,
kilt-like skirt with one end over left shoulder. *Brass*
with blurred features.
Height 0.146 m Width 0.073 m
McLellan Galleries, 8; Weidner 1951, 137; Seeden
1978, 22, Pl VIII.18; 1980, 34 n 21.
Acquired W. Williams, 1948.

Seeden has shown that this is a forged copy of a
well known second millennium BC figure
probably from Syria and now in the Louvre
(Seeden 1978, 22–4). She concludes that the
forger must have had the original in hand, reproduced a model and took a mould from it to
make duplicates. Analysis supports her conclusions (Appendix A).

119 Decorated Slab 28.34

Unprovenanced

Rectangular slab with central quadruped facing a
plant to right and on its back a bird attacked by a
snake which reaches up from its coiled tail on the
basal border. Coarse *stone.*
Height 0.365 m Length 0.469 m
Unpublished.
Acquired W. Williams, 1948.

Small stone slabs with cursorily rendered scenes
were used to decorate the walls of public structures at such Syrian sites as Guzana (Tell Halaf)
in the first millennium BC. They have neither
a border on all sides as here nor compositions
such as this.

120 Sceptre 28.39

Unprovenanced.

Rod with spherical and pointed terminals and three
globular rings with moulded terminals placed on the
rod. Probably *bronze.*
Length 0.527 m.
Unpublished.
Acquired W. Williams, 1949.

The upper part of the rod, near the spherical
terminal, does not match the lower part. This
may be a pastiche, with affinities to the plainer
sceptres depicted on Neo-Assyrian reliefs (*cf*
Hrouda 1965, Pl 32.1–8).

121 Animal Figurine 28.40

Unprovenanced.

Roughly finished animal with large head in relation
to cubical body. Head consists of long muzzle with
socketed eyes and upright ears tilted forwards. Body
stamped with circular stamps bearing cross motif.
Legs are no more than short grooved stubs. *Gold.*
Length 0.028 m Width 0.007 m
Unpublished
Acquired G.F. Williams 1949.

118

119

120

122

121

123

122 Ram-Headed Terminal 28.50

Unprovenanced.

Crowning a short socketed sleeve are the foreparts of two recumbent rams with their beards extending onto chests. Over their joined backs is a bordered saddlecloth with decorated horizontal registers. Cast and traced *bronze*.

Height 0.053 m Width 0.076 m
Unpublished.

Acquired Spink & Son, 1952.

This is probably west Iranian since it is there that the concept of animals joined in this fashion was well known (*cf* Pope 1938, IV, Pl 17 C). It is most evident in the column capitals at Persepolis. Saddlecloths were also depicted on zoomorphic pottery vessels. The absence of good parallels and the analyses which reveal the presence of moderate levels of lead in the copper alloy urge caution in accepting it as ancient metalwork (see Appendix A).

123 Animal Figurine 28.51

Unprovenanced.

Standing figure with long flat head, horns joined at tips, strong shoulders, short extended tail and straight legs, each pair joined at the feet. Traced lines on the mane and tail, ovals on shoulders, arcs on shoulders and haunches, diamonds on upper legs. Cast and traced *copper-tin-zinc* alloy.

Height 0.088 m Length 0.112 m
Unpublished.

Acquired Spink & Son, 1952.

This alloy has sufficiently high levels of zinc to indicate that it is not an ancient metalwork (see Appendix A).

124 Boat Model 28.55

Unprovenanced.

Boat with central convex canopy decorated in relief with stamped rosettes and concentric diamonds and circles, the motifs set inside angular areas defined by raised borders. A line of rosettes above the keel. *Terracotta*.

Height 0.04 m Length 0.15 m
Exh. Glasgow 1949, No. 107.

Acquired Peter Wilson, 1948.

This is perhaps from Mesopotamia, Seleucid or later.

125 Seated Figure 28.63

Unprovenanced.

Figure with flexed legs, arms extended and wearing a cylindrical headdress with floral terminal. Extensively patched up, many features such as possible anklets and bosses at the base of the headdress are now indistinct. *Brass arms and, possibly, body*.

Height 0.194 Width 0.036 m
Unpublished.

Acquired G.F. Williams, 1951.

This is a slightly larger copy of a later second millennium BC Syrian seated figure now in the Louvre (Pritchard 1954, No. 466). The Louvre example clearly shows that the figure was meant to have pronounced bosses on the headdress, rings in large ears, incised brows, necklace with double spiral pendant, right hand extended upwards and sandals. X-rays reveal major discontinuities between the head and torso and between the hips and knees. Parts are definitely made of brass (Appendix A) and so it may be a pastiche with modern elements added, or entirely false.

126 Smiting God Figure 28.64

Allegedly from Ras Shamra-Ugarit, Syria.

Striding male with horned headdress, pierced, lug-shaped ears, right arm raised, left extended, wearing a short, belted kilt and standing on a rectilinear base with attached square-sectioned tenon under the left foot. *Bronze*.

Height 0.412 m Width 0.14 m
McLellan Galleries, 8; Weidner 1951, 137 Hannah 1953, 300–1, Fig 2; Culican 1961, 141, Fig 14; James 1965, 197, ill 99.

Acquired G.F. Williams, 1952.

Many types of metal figures were produced in the Levant, and this conforms in general terms with the smiting god type of the later second millennium BC. Characteristic examples are portrayed in an Egyptianizing style with elaborate headdresses and short skirt, right arm raised to brandish a spear, left one extended to hold another object and one leg in front of the other with often one or two tenons extending directly from the feet. Evidence from Byblos suggests that some were probably placed in altar niches;

others may have formed part of composite scenes (Seeden 1980, No. 1725 and Pl 133.3).

This example can be singled out from the broad range of Levantine figures primarily by its large size, awkwardly rendered shoulders, short forearms and basal plate arrangement. During the Late Bronze Age its exceptional size is approached only by the famous 'Ingot God' from Enkomi in Cyprus (Height 35 cms) which also has relatively short forearms, a pair of small bosses on the chest and large horns (Seeden 1980, No. 1794). As on other figures that are fixed to a metal base plate, the tenon is placed centrally below the 'Ingot God'. The Burrell smiting god would seem to be unique in originally possessing two widely spaced tenons extending from a base plate, but this could be explained by the fact that its exceptional size required an additional tenon for stability. Almost all tenons on figures with base plates are round-sectioned and even those with rectangular sections are much shorter and more coarsely finished than this (re-worked?) example (*cf ibid* No 1725).

Only a few figures have projecting horns and as these are often broken this well preserved set may be compared to the large examples on the 'Baal' stele from Ugarit (*ibid* Pl 136.1) or the even larger pair on the unique Horned God from Enkomi (*PK* 14, Pl 468 b). Another slight oddity is the manner in which the kilt belt follows the outline of the body rather than standing out as a vertical-sided projection, more securely clasping the waist than sliding along the hips as here (*cf* Seeden 1980, Nos. 1690, 1694, 1823).

Yet by themselves these atypical features are insufficient to reject the sculpture outright. Other features are perfectly normal. The conical helmet with disc-shaped top that rises straight from the head without a border has parallels (*ibid* No. 1758) as does the plain kilt (*ibid* No. 1737), though in view of the figure's size, it is surprising that no fold or decoration is shown. Ears are normally rounded, but again similar squared ears are known (*ibid* Nos. 1784, 1789). The earrings are missing from the perforations of the Burrell smiting god, but as they may have been of precious metal like silver (*ibid* No 1761), this is understandable. The fists are also perforated and since forgers often leave them unpierced, they are an argument for the authenticity of the work.

124

125

126

Given the frequency with which smiting god figures have been forged (see Seeden 1978), full metallographic analysis is warranted. Surface analyses suggest nothing untoward (Appendices A and B).

127 Decorated Palette 28.69

Unprovenanced.

Flat rectangular slab with rounded terminals and two depressions in top surface. Edges incised with continuous band of hatched festoons. *Stone*.
Length 0.087 m Width 0.044m
Unpublished.
Acquired G.F. Williams, 1953.

Cosmetic palettes of this type are characteristic of Early Minoan Crete (*cf* Xanthoudides 1924, Pl 24.679–80). Although decorated Cretan stonework such as an elaborate lamp has been found in Western Asia, it is of a different type and later in date.

128 Dagger Handle 33.107

Unprovenanced.

Handle with expanded terminal, studded handgrip and elaborate socket with relief decoration of Xs set in squares, projecting filled rings and flat studs and four prongs extending along the missing blade. Possibly cast *bronze*.
Length 0.185 m
McLellan Galleries 12, right ill.
Acquired W. Williams, 1948.

This is probably an ethnographic article rather than a Luristan bronze as in *McLellan Galleries* 12, right.

129 Lamp Stand 33.184

Unprovenanced.

Socketed cylinder set on dish, the cylinder with mouldings, spirally decorated base and two opposed vertical handles. *Bronze*.
Height 0.23 m Diameter 0.165 m
Unpublished.
Acquired G.F. Williams, 1952.

This is probably Persian, of the 12th century AD (*cf* Pope 1938, VI, Pl 1283 D).

130 Goat-Headed Terminal 33.192

Unprovenanced.

Bearded goat forequarters with short horns, naturalistically rendered beard, raised forelegs truncated at joints, rectilinear-sectioned socketed body with moulded rim. Probably *bronze*.
Height 0.135 m Width 0.054 m
Unpublished.
Acquired A. Garabed, 1952.

The realism of the goat is akin to that of a billy goat figurine attributed to Roman production of the 3rd century AD (Kozloff *et al* 1986, 54.154). Its deep, sturdy socket further suggests that, rather than simply a finial for a decorative piece, the terminal might have belonged to a robust utilitarian object.

131 Spouted Jug 33.210

Unprovenanced.

Disc-based jug with globular body, wide cylindrical neck, flat everted rim folded over and elongated, right-angled spout secured to the shoulder by twelve bosses with wires passed through the body and splayed on the interior. Traced, stylized face on bulbous base of spout. *Silver* with *bronze(?)* wire.
Height 0.096 m Diameter 0.232 m
Sotheby's 16.1.1956, 12.87; Moorey 1971, 280.
Acquired F. Partridge, 1956.

Signs of lathe working on the base suggest that this is a modern copy of a well known Luristan bronze type of the 8th–7th centuries BC (*cf* Moorey 1971, 280). The face on the base of the spout is stylized like those on bronze and pottery jugs (*cf* Boehmer 1965, 815–820, Figs 5–7).

[Note: The 'Assyro-Persian' marble relief in *McLellan Galleries* 11 is no longer in the collection]

127

128

130

131

129

Appendix A: Surface Analysis of Metals
Paul Wilthew

Introduction

Forty-two of the objects included in the catalogue were selected for analysis. This was required both to allow a more accurate description of the objects in the catalogue and in some cases to help decide the authenticity of the objects. In order to assess the authenticity of the objects the results were compared to published analytical data (Branigan 1974, Moorey 1971, Moorey 1985).

The objects had layers of corrosion products on the surfaces, and had been subjected to unknown post-excavation treatments. The surface layers are described as 'corrosion' or 'corroded' below, although they may include substances applied post-recovery. No study was made of the composition of the layers.

Method

As the composition of the surface layers was uncertain, and because the techniques used involved surface analysis, reliable quantitative data could only be obtained if the surface deposits were removed. In most cases this was not acceptable to J.K. Thomson, the curator responsible for the objects, but small areas of a few objects were cleaned to base metal for quantitative analysis. Cleaning was by abrasion using silicon carbide paper (1000 grade) or by scraping with a new scalpel blade. It was not possible to polish these areas and therefore the geometry of the areas analysed, particularly by x-ray fluorescence, was uncertain. The cleaning carried out was the minimum necessary to reveal the base metal, and it is possible that some depletion of elements due to corrosion had occurred even in the cleaned areas analysed.

Despite the presence of these possible sources of error in the results, they should give a reasonable estimate of the original base metal composition of the alloys.

Two analytical techniques were used:

1 *Energy dispersive x-ray fluorescence* (XRF)

Selected areas on all objects were irradiated by a primary x-ray beam collimated to give a beam diameter of approximately 1.5 mm on the object's surface. The primary beam was produced using a Rhodium target x-ray tube run at 46 keV. Fluorescence x-rays were detected using a Si (Li) detector and recorded into a 2048 channel multichannel analyser prior to storage on disc.

The areas analysed were those which appeared least contaminated with surface deposits. Wherever possible cleaned areas were used, otherwise the area where the corrosion products appeared to be thinnest was selected.

Quantitative results for some cleaned areas were obtained using the fundamental parameters program FUNBAT, similar to that described by Cowell (1977), calibrated with pure element standards.

2 *Scanning electron microscopy with energy dispersive microanalysis* (EDX)

Cleaned areas of the smaller objects were analysed quantitatively using a Link Analytical AN10000 system with Si (Li) detector attached to a Camscan series 4 scanning electron microscope. Only areas observed to be corrosion free were analysed on each object. The objects were irradiated using a 20 KeV electron beam, and the spectra were collected over 100 seconds.

Quantitative results were obtained using Link Systems ZAF-4 program with virtual standards.

Results

A list of the elements present in each area, based on XRF analyses with the single exception of the rivet through **105**, is given in Table 3 and the quantitative results are listed in Table 4.

The relative concentrations of major and minor elements in corrosion products does not necessarily reflect their relative concentrations in the original base metal and trace elements present in the base metal may not be detectable in corroded surfaces. Contamination of corroded surfaces is also a problem and in the present work iron was almost certainly a contaminant in all uncleaned surfaces, although it was probably also present as a trace in the base metal of most, if not all, objects, and in two cases (**40** and **99**) it was present at fairly high levels. Manganese was also detected in some corroded surfaces, but was assumed to be a contaminant and its presence was not recorded. Some apparent inconsistencies between the quantitative EDX results and the qualitative XRF results for minor and trace elements in the same objects were found, but as different areas were being analysed and the XRF analyses probably included corrosion products some differences would be expected. The detection limit for the EDX analyses was also higher than for XRF.

Discussion

30, 40, 80, 85   These four objects were the earliest in date of those analysed (*c* 2000 BC or earlier). As might be expected (Pickles 1988) they include the two arsenical copper alloys found during this work (**40**, **80**) and the compositions of the other objects, copper (**30**) and copper-tin-arsenic alloy (**85**) were also consistent with an early date. Arsenic was only detected above trace levels in one later object (**61**) discussed below.

43   A bronze figurine. Its composition was consistent with its date.

60   This Urartian bull's head gave similar results to the Luristan bronzes above and its composition is consistent with its date. An apparent patch in the top of its head contained a trace of silver which was not detected in the head itself, and the tin content was higher, but the surface of the object was corroded and the differences may not be significant.

61   This finial and base from Luristan did not conform to the compositional pattern found for most Luristan objects (see **64**). The two components, although both bronze, were of quite different composition. The finial contained relatively high levels of antimony, whereas the base was low in antimony, but contained high levels of lead and arsenic. The tin content of the base was probably also higher. The finial is fairly close in composition to the group of Luristan bronzes described below, the only difference being a relatively high antimony content, but the base is of quite different composition.

The differences between the two components raise questions as to whether they were originally both part of the same object, and the differences between the composition of other Luristan bronzes and this object may raise doubts about its authenticity. The analytical evidence suggests but cannot prove, that the two components were not original parts of the same object, and that although the finial is probably authentic the authenticity of the base should be questioned.

64,65, 67, 70, 72, 73,74,76, 78, 79, 81,82, 83, 84, 86, 88, 90   These objects, all from Luristan or Iran, were all bronzes of similar composition. The tin content undoubtedly varied but quantitative analysis of five of the objects suggested that it was probably about 5%–12% tin in most cases. The alloys all contained traces of arsenic and lead, but silver was not detectable. Antimony and nickel were detectable in some objects. Compositionally, these objects formed a (broad) group and the analytical results are quite consistent with their dates (ranging between c 1300 BC and c 400 BC). The results are comparable with those of Moorey (1971) who found the majority of Luristan bronzes to have between 4% and 13% tin and that traces of nickel, lead and arsenic were common, and traces of antimony occurred in some objects.

Different components from the same object gave very similar readings, including the pair of cheekpieces (74).

69 This pin terminal appeared, visually, to have a white metal surface on the front, thought to be tin plating on the surface of a lower tin copper alloy base metal (H. McKerrell, unpublished work). Analysis of the front did show a higher tin content than a cleaned area on the back of the object, but even the back contained 26% tin. This suggests that the base metal itself is a high tin bronze (the only example in the present work) and that the white surface may be due to tin enrichment.

70, 72, 73, 74, 76, 78, 79 – *See* 64

80 *See* 30

81, 82, 83, 84 – *See* 64

85 – *See* 30

86 – *See* 64

87 A libation vessel of quite high purity silver, comparable with that of the foil in 96. Its composition is consistent with its date.

88 *See* 64

89 A copper vase. Apart from iron no trace elements were detected in the copper in marked contrast to all the other copper alloy objects analysed. The high purity of the metal is not sufficient to prove that this object does not date from c 400 BC, particularly as the method used is not very sensitive. However, the unusual composition of the vase must cast some doubt on its authenticity.

90 *See* 64

91 This amphora had been extensively restored and was x-radiographed to identify the position of several modern metal patches in the body of the amphora. The original metal in the body of the amphora appeared to have completely corroded, although handle and spout both contained a substantial metallic core. The three components were each of different composition, although none was inconsistent with the date of the object. The analytical results do not support the hypothesis that the three components are all original parts of the same object, but they cannot disprove it. Examination of the object showed that both the handle and spout had been attached or re-attached relatively recently.

96 The axe-head was a heavily corroded bronze, with silver foil. The silver was quite pure, although the surface analysed may have been depleted in copper due to corrosion. The purity of the silver was similar to that of the libation vessel, 87.

97 The composition of this object, leaded bronze, is consistent with its date although in the present work leaded alloys were rare, the only other example being 122, and parallels with the object are copper with a hollow filled with lead. The objects were used as weights and 97 is of similar weight to other examples suggesting that it is authentic. It was, however produced by a more sophisticated method than other examples in that the correct average density was achieved by introducing lead into the alloy rather than plugging with lead after casting, although final adjustment of the weight could have been made by removal of metal after casting, provided it was not too low.

98   A bronze bull partially plated with silver. The analytical results are consistent with the date of the object.

99   A bronze object whose composition is quite consistent with its date. The iron content is quite high, but the significance of this is difficult to assess as both ore and flux can be the source of iron in unrefined copper (Craddock & Meeks 1987). The high iron content is probably the result of using unrefined copper, but does not necessarily imply that an iron rich ore was used.

100   One eye of this wooden head contained an inlay of uncertain composition within which was a pupil also of unknown material. Analysis of the eye and pupil confirmed, as expected, that they were not metallic. Examination of the pupil suggested that it might be organic, perhaps wood, but the similarity of the analyses of the pupil and the wooden head itself should not be taken as evidence for this as only contaminants were detected. Visually the inlay appeared pale and inhomogeneous on a fracture surface and XRF showed it to be calcium rich. It seems probable that the inlay is a mineral, probably containing calcium carbonate or calcium sulphate perhaps mixed with sand.

105   A bronze bull's head with a copper rich rivet through a hole in one corner. The rivet probably contained low levels of arsenic, lead and tin, but some contamination from the head itself, particularly with tin, was possible.

111, 112, 118, 123, 125   Each of these objects contained significant levels of zinc which cast doubt on its authenticity. Traces of zinc can be introduced accidentally into copper during smelting if zinc-containing ores are used (Tylecote 1977) and therefore a trace of zinc in an early copper alloy object is not an indication that it is a fake. However genuine brasses are rare, although not unknown, before the Roman period (Craddock 1978, Craddock 1980) and the presence of a high zinc content in a pre-Roman object must cast doubt on its authenticity. In the present work, three objects, two brasses (**112, 118**) and one copper-tin-zinc alloy (**123**) contained sufficiently high zinc levels to suggest that they were probably not authentic.

125 is a more complex object. The arms are brass and therefore probably not authentic, but the zinc level in the head, body and leg areas was lower. However, only corroded surfaces could be analysed and the zinc content in the base metal may be higher than in the surface layers. It is probably correct to assume that the object is not authentic, but the possibility that some parts may be genuine cannot be completely ruled out.

The silver vessel, **111**, also contained zinc, at a relatively low concentration (0.9%). However, assuming that the zinc was introduced to the silver as a copper-zinc alloy with the 16.1% copper in the silver, the copper alloy would have contained a minimum of 5% zinc, which suggests that an early date is unlikely.

122   Apart from objects identified as probable fakes, this was one of very few copper alloy objects containing more than a trace of lead. Although its composition is not obviously inconsistent with an early date, leaded alloys were not commonly used for similar objects (Moorey 1985). There is no reason to assume that the object is not genuine purely on analytical grounds, but if its authenticity is questionable on stylistic or other grounds, the analytical results could support the conclusion that it is not authentic.

123, 125 – *See* **111**

126   A bronze figure. Its composition was consistent with its alleged date.

Table 3: Results of surface analysis of selected objects in the catalogue.

Key: tr = trace   +++ = major element
nd = not detected   ++ = detected at moderate levels
? = possibly present   + = detected at lower levels
(A) = analysed area was abraded to base metal.

Cat	Description	Area	Fe	Co	Ni	Cu	Zn	As	Au	Pb	Ag	Sn	Sb
30	Foundation Figurine (A)		tr	nd	tr	+++	nd	tr	nd	tr	?	tr	?
40	Foundation Figurine		+	nd	tr	+++	tr	+	nd	?	nd	nd	tr
43	Supplicant Figurine		tr	nd	tr	+++	nd	tr	nd	tr	tr	++	nd
60	Bull's head (A)	Head	tr	nd	nd	+++	nd	tr	nd	tr	nd	+	tr
61	Standard	Top	tr	nd	tr	+++	nd	tr	nd	tr	?	+	+
		Base	tr	nd	tr	+++	nd	+	nd	+	?	+	tr
64	Standard (A)		tr	nd	tr	+++	nd	tr	nd	tr	nd	+	tr
65	Tube		tr	nd	nd	+++	nd	tr	nd	tr	tr	+	tr
67	Zoomorphic Figurine (A)		tr	nd	nd	+++	nd	tr	nd	tr	nd	++	tr
69	Pin Terminal	Front	tr	nd	nd	+++	nd	tr	nd	tr	nd	++	nd
	(A)	Back	tr	nd	nd	+++	nd	tr	nd	tr	nd	++	nd
70	Pin Head	Head	tr	nd	tr	+++	nd	tr	nd	tr	nd	+	nd
		Shank	+++	nd	nd	tr	nd	nd	nd	nd	nd	tr	nd
72	Horse Bit	Left horse	tr	nd	nd	+++	nd	tr	nd	tr	nd	+	nd
		Right horse	tr	nd	tr	+++	nd	tr	nd	tr	nd	+	nd
		Bar	tr	nd	tr	+++	nd	tr	nd	tr	nd	+	nd
73	Horse Bit	Left horse	tr	nd	nd	+++	nd	tr	nd	tr	nd	+	nd
		Right horse	tr	nd	?	+++	nd	tr	nd	tr	?	+	?
		Bar	tr	nd	?	+++	nd	tr	nd	tr	nd	+	nd
74	Cheek-piece		tr	nd	nd	+++	nd	tr	nd	tr	nd	++	nd
76	Harness Ring		tr	nd	tr	+++	nd	tr	nd	tr	nd	++	nd
78	Whetstone Handle		tr	nd	tr	+++	nd	tr	nd	tr	nd	tr	nd
79	Whetstone Handle		tr	nd	tr	+++	nd	tr	nd	tr	nd	+	nd
80	Pick-head		tr	?	tr	+++	nd	+	nd	tr	nd	nd	nd
81	Axe-head (A)		tr	nd	?	+++	nd	?	nd	tr	nd	+	nd
82	Axe-head		tr	nd	tr	+++	nd	tr	nd	tr	nd	+	tr
83	Axe-head (A)		tr	nd	tr	+++	nd	tr	nd	tr	nd	+	tr

No.	Item	Part											
84	Axe-head		tr	nd	nd	+++	nd	tr	nd	tr	nd	+	tr
85	Macehead (A)		tr	nd	tr	+++	nd	+	+	nd	tr	+	tr
86	Dagger		tr	nd	tr	+++	nd	tr	tr	nd	tr	+	?
87	Libation Beaker (also bismuth) (A)		nd	nd	nd	+	nd	nd	tr	+++	tr	nd	nd
88	Jar		tr	nd	tr	+++	nd	tr	tr	nd	tr	+	tr
89	Flask (A)		tr	?	?	+++	nd	nd	nd	nd	nd	nd	tr
90	Bowl		tr	nd	tr	+++	nd	tr	tr	tr	tr	+	tr
91	Amphora	Body	tr	nd	tr	+++	?	tr	tr	nd	tr	+	nd
		Spout	tr	nd	?	+++	nd	tr	tr	nd	tr	+	nd
		Handle	tr	nd	nd	+++	nd	+	tr	nd	tr	+	nd
96	Fenestrated Axe-head	Axe	tr	nd	nd	+++	nd	tr	tr	tr	tr	+	tr
		Foil	tr	nd	nd	+	?	+	tr	+++	tr	+++	nd
97	Bull Weight (A)		tr	nd	tr	+++	nd	++	nd	nd	++	nd	nd
98	Bull Figurine (A)	Base metal	tr	nd	tr	+++	nd	+	+	tr	+	tr	tr
		Coating	+	nd	tr	++	nd	tr	+	+++	tr	+++	nd
99	Bull Figurine (A)		+	nd	tr	+++	nd	tr	nd	nd	+	nd	nd
105	Bull's Head (A)		tr	nd	nd	+++	nd	tr	nd	nd	+	tr	tr
		Rivet	tr	nd	nd	+++	+	tr	nd	nd	+	nd	nd
111	Vessel (A)		tr	nd	tr	++	+	tr	tr	+	+	+	nd
112	Armlet		tr	nd	tr	+++	++	nd	nd	nd	tr	tr	nd
118	Figure		tr	nd	tr	+++	++	tr	+	tr	+	+	nd
122	Ram-Headed Terminal		tr	nd	nd	+++	nd	++	tr	nd	++	tr	tr
123	Animal Figurine (A)		tr	nd	tr	+++	+	+	tr	nd	+	tr	tr
125	Seated figure	Left arm	tr	nd	tr	+++	++	+	nd	nd	+	+	tr
		Headdress	tr	nd	tr	+++	+	tr	tr	nd	tr	+	tr
126	Figure		tr	?	tr	++	nd	tr	tr	nd	tr	+	?

Appendix A · 153

Table 4: Quantititative analytical results.

Key: nd = not detected

: na = not analysed for

*This object also contained a trace of bismuth.

Cat.	Method	Fe	Ni	Cu	Zn	As	Au	Pb	Ag	Sn	Sb
30	EDX	<0.1	<0.1	99.3	nd	<0.1	nd	0.4	<0.1	0.2	0.2
60	XRF	0.3	nd	89.1	nd	1.1	nd	0.3	<0.1	9.0	0.2
64	EDX	0.4	0.1	91.1	nd	0.5	nd	1.9	0.2	5.9	<0.1
67	EDX	0.2	nd	90.6	nd	<0.1	nd	0.1	nd	9.0	<0.1
69	EDX	0.2	nd	73.2	nd	<0.1	nd	0.5	nd	26.1	nd
82	EDX	<0.1	0.3	91.3	nd	<0.1	nd	0.4	nd	8.0	<0.1
83	EDX	0.1	0.4	90.0	nd	0.2	nd	1.1	nd	8.2	<0.1
85	XRF	0.3	<0.1	87.7	nd	2.5	nd	4.0	0.1	5.3	0.1
87*	XRF	nd	nd	2.5	nd	nd	0.4	1.2	95.9	nd	nd
90	EDX	0.3	0.3	86.3	nd	0.4	nd	1.1	nd	11.7	<0.1
96 (foil)	EDX	0.3	nd	1.7	nd	nd	<0.1	1.7	96.3	nd	nd
97	EDX	0.1	0.1	81.3	nd	0.6	nd	10.1	nd	7.8	nd
98	EDX	0.2	<0.1	90.5	nd	0.1	nd	0.1	0.3	8.7	<0.1
99	EDX	2.0	0.1	86.6	nd	0.3	nd	0.9	nd	10.4	nd
105	EDX	<0.1	nd	89.0	nd	0.5	nd	<0.1	<0.1	10.4	<0.1
105 (rivet)	EDX	0.2	nd	97.2	nd	0.9	nd	0.7	nd	1.1	nd
111	XRF	na	na	16.1	0.9	<0.1	0.5	0.9	81.6	nd	nd

Appendix B: Metal Analyses

Excepting 126, the objects listed here were analyzed in the Württembergisches Landesmuseum's Arbeitsgemeinschaft für Metallurgie des Altertums through the good offices of S. Junghans with additional notes kindly supplied by Dr. A. Hartmann. The spectral analytical technique employed is described by S. Junghans, H. Klein, and E. Scheufele in the 34th *Bericht der Römische – Germanischen Kommission* 1954: 77 ff. Prof. Ellwood of the Department of Metallurgy at the Royal College of Science and Technology at Hamilton, Scotland carried out the chemical and spectroscopic analysis of 126.

Table 5: Metal Analyses

Catalogue Number	Burrell Coll. No.	Lab. Code	Sn	Pb	As	Sb	Ag	Ni	Bi	Au	Zn	Co	Fe	Cu
40	28.75	9330	Sp	0.61	0.8	~0.02	0.17	0.29	0	Sp	0	0.02	+	N.R.
43	28.54		~5.9	0.2	0.93	~0.03	0.27	0.35	0	0	0	0.06	+	N.R.
96	28.72	:9332	~4.9	0.69	1.25	0.04	0.26	0.06	Sp	0	0	0	+	N.R.
97	28.30	9326	~8.8	> 5	0.25	0.07	0.12	0.12	0.008	0	0	0	+	N.R.
99	28.31	*9329	~6.5	Sp	0.54	0.02	<0.01	0.02	0	0	0	0.06	++	N.R.
105	28.62	9327	~7.5	0.07	0.1	0.18	0.1	~0.01	0.007	0	0	0	+	N.R.
126	28.64		13.74	1.46	0		0			0			0.13	84.4

~ = approximately

Sp = trace (Spur/Spuren)

N.R. = not recorded

: = Analysis of the bronze only. Traces of electrum were noted, presumably in the foil.

* = Strongly magnetic

Concordance of Burrell Collection Numbers with Catalogue Numbers

COLL. NO.	CAT. NO.	COLL. NO.	CAT. NO.	COLL. NO.	CAT. NO.
				28.79	111
13.230	100	28.36	33	28.80	21
19.26	104	28.37	42	28.81	44
19.43	103	28.38	49	28.82	59
19.70	102	28.39	120	28.83	95
19.91	101	28.40	121	28.84	94
19.110	113	28.41	14	28.85	109
19.135	107	28.42	98	28.86	108
19.145	106	28.43	93	33.85	66
19.152	110	28.44	89	33.88	63
28.1	22	28.45	16	33.89	62
28.2	15	28.46	57	33.90	64
28.3	29	28.47	56	33.92	65
28.4	23	28.48	20	33.93	76
28.5	25	28.49	18	33.94	71
28.6	28	28.50	122	33.97	86
28.7	27	28.51	123	33.102	83
28.8	19	28.52	54	33.103	82
28.9	114	28.53	41	33.104	80
28.10	39	28.54	43	33.105	69
28.11	26	28.55	124	33.106	73
28.12	38	28.56	13	33.107	128
28.13	115	28.57	3	33.108	70
28.14	17	28.58	2	33.109	81
28.15	31	28.59	5	33.110	88
28.16	37	28.60	4	33.111	72
28.17	9	28.61	50	33.112	85
28.18	1	28.62	105	33.113	90
28.19	11	28.63	125	33.176	77
28.20	12	28.64	126	33.177	75
28.21	58	28.65	51	33.178/9	74
28.22	10	28.66	32	33.180	61
28.23	35	28.67	36	33.181	68
28.24	34	28.68	6	33.184	129
28.25	7	28.69	127	33.190	84
28.26	8	28.70	48	33.191	112
28.27-8	116-117	28.71	24	33.192	130
28.29	30	28.72	96	33.209	79
28.30	97	28.73	52	33.210	131
28.31	99	28.74	55	33.211	78
28.32	118	28.75	40	33.212	60
28.33	47	28.76	67	33.213	92
28.34	119	28.77	53	33.214	91
28.35	45	28.78	46	33.215	87